I'M STILL STANDING

by

Lee Evans

BMP

Blue Mendos Publications

Published by Blue Mendos Publications

In association with Amazon KDP Publishing

Published in paperback 2023

Category: Life Story & Memoirs

Copyright Lee Evans © 2023

ISBN : 9798859245390

Cover design by Jill Rinaldi © 2023

DEDICATION

To my mum and Ginge.

Mum, you ripped up the guide book for Duchenne's parents and wrote your own. I owe you everything.

Ginge, you went head to head with the condition and never backed down.
Love you brother.

ACKNOWLEDGEMENTS

I would like to thank Dean and Jill Rinaldi for their patience and professional opinion with helping me complete this book. I'd really hit a wall with this project but their constant support and good advice got me over the line.

I have an army of friends who have supported me so much in life. It's impossible for me to thank you all by name but your encouragement and love has got me through many dark days.

A nod to P.H. for keeping me sane every day and always checking up on me.

Four important, special, friends have spurred me on: Danny Hogan, Marc Fevrier, Jan Steil and Jodie Kempster. Friendship that knows no boundaries.

Family have been my launch pad to get here. Two people stand out. My Uncle Shugs, a kind, genuine man who has always been there through all the crap situations. Every family needs an Uncle Shugs. The other is my Uncle Billy. A man who's an expert on everything but without having a clue about the subject. He's a hero to me who fights my corner all of the time. Thanks for everything Uncle Bill.

Millwall Football Club. It isn't just a team. It's part of your life and an addiction in many ways. It's given me something to focus on since childhood. From the top table in the Boardroom to fans on the terraces, thank you, but most of all thank you to the chaps for treating me like any other lad.

So many carers have pushed me on and helped me achieve my goals.

There's been a few charlatans, but the ones who've always put my welfare first are priceless. So, the long term who have had the patience and mental strength to put up with me, thank you. Sam White, Billy Bradford and Helen Brown, I owe you so much. Thank you again.

The Lane Fox Unit are a team of skilled professionals who have been committed to keeping me on track and giving me an opportunity to achieve my dreams. Professor Hart, who you will have gathered by now, is a very special person in my life, and with the help of his team has put me back together many, many times. Dr Murphy is the man with the plan and his wise words have got me through some challenging days. I've been looked after by some amazing doctors and again I can't thank them all, but I have to thank two more. Dr Suh and Dr Marino, your humour and positivity while acknowledging we're up shit creek is a priceless skill.

Kelly Stewart and Natalie Grey are two amazing nurses who should be running the NHS. They're Old School nurses with compassion and have so much knowledge. They have kept my feet on the ground for years.

Father David Lambert came into my life when my brother died and I was at an all-time low, and just knowing he is there for us all keeps me sane during dark times.

My Mum: Anyone who met my mum will say that she was the most inspirational person they knew. Giving up was never an option for her boys. You were allowed to cry but not give up. You gave me the tools and mindset to say fuck you Muscular Dystrophy, I'll give you a run for your money.

She was simply the best.

Ginge, my brother, thank you for being the voice of reason and keeping us out of trouble; it didn't always work, but we got there in the end. I think of you every day and by missing you I understand the importance of life and appreciate it. I know how lucky I am to have had the opportunities that you never had.

If it wasn't for my amazing wife Kellie I wouldn't be here today. She's helped me so much with this book too. You know when to cuddle me and tell me I've got this and when to put a rocket up my arse and tell me to sort myself out. It's a truly priceless gift. You've morphed into my mum. There are tears for a few minutes during a struggle, then you're taking on the world.

I never believed I would fall in love like this, but you stole my heart. Please keep it for ever.

My amazing prince, my boy, Jude. You've sparked an energy source I never knew I had and you're my world. I always wanted to be a dad, but now I know I only ever wanted to be your dad. Every day you make me smile and laugh. You're my treat to myself, my medication. Thank you for finding the hidden desire in me when I was on the ropes.

Blimey I'm like Barry McGuigan thanking the world when he won his Featherweight title.

Right, that's your lot.

What more do you want for a cockle per book?

Be Lucky,

Lee x

FOREWORD BY KELLIE EVANS

I told Lee for a long time that he could help others living with his condition, whether it be having the illness or living with someone who has it. He protested for so long and I was surprised when he announced he was writing this book. I felt he had so much to give to others and could help in a way which he didn't believe. I think a big part of helping others is having to look at yourself first and it wasn't something that Lee was prepared to do for a long time, but I feel he has come full circle in life and is now able to share his experiences with a view to even helping one other person.

It's true what he says..........

When I met him, I saw a funny bloke (or so he thought) who was handsome, genuine and knew right from wrong. I never saw the chair, obstacles or, more importantly, Muscular Dystrophy.

And I still don't.

When Jude came along, it changed him in so many ways; ranging from believing he wasn't just another number on the DMD list, to empowering him to keep going. "Fighting like a cornered lion", as he puts it. Listening to him and Jude is priceless and fills me with pride. Two individuals who are spectacular in their own way. One who thought he would never meet the other and one who will never quite understand his role in the other's life.

He is Lee, my amazing husband and the father of my boy.

We have been through so much together and it's only made us stronger, so in some ways I would never change history. We couldn't anyway, so there is no point pondering over it.

INTRODUCTION

So why are you reading this? I am not too sure really. Nothing overly amazing has ever happened to me.

I didn't score the winner for England in a World Cup Final and I haven't found the cure for some terrible disease either. I am just a bloke off the estate who loves a beer, supports Millwall Football Club, settled down and got married, and then got the best job in the world. Being a dad.

Why anyone would care about how I got here is anyone's guess, so, if someone has given you this to read as a present you might want to chuck it back at them. But then again there are a lot of nosey people out there, so maybe you want to give it a try.

I would never have dreamed of writing all this down until a few years ago when I spent a day meeting MPs and big wigs from the Muscular Dystrophy group. The meeting took place at Portcullis House in London with the Houses of Parliament as a back drop. I had never attended any disability focus groups or meetings linked to Muscular Dystrophy and after attending this one I felt vindicated. I only attended this one because I had been kept in hospital for an extra six weeks by NHS red tape and wanted to bend some ears as I had a bee in my bonnet about it all. The hope of finding a free bar also enticed me to attend, but I was left disappointed.

When I entered the room where the meeting was being held, I was shocked by how depressed everyone seemed. Of course, this wasn't meant to be a jolly up and the whole business of Duchenne Muscular Dystrophy is totally sad and heart wrenching, but it doesn't have to always be like that. You are allowed to have some enjoyment; actually, it's imperative to grab some positives from what is a negative situation.

Straight away the meeting had random family members speaking about what a terrible condition Muscular Dystrophy is. Now, that's all well and good, but when you have a room full of people sitting there living with the condition, surely they are better placed to speak about it? I mean you wouldn't get Hugh Heffner's chauffeur do a speech on shagging playmates while Heff is plonked in the corner eating a sausage roll, would you?

Then the bit that really got me to put all this down on paper was this. A young lady in her late 20s (a bit of a sort actually) got up and spoke about how that week her son had been diagnosed with Duchenne Muscular Dystrophy. She said that she was "prepared" for him not to be able to go to school, make friends, go on holidays or really have any decent quality of life. I wanted to scream "NO!". I wanted to tell her that's not true, and I wanted to tell her about scrapes me and my brother got into. The ugly birds we have pulled, shitty northern football grounds I have visited, and the long and boring days at work I had to endure. The woman was whisked away pretty quickly so I didn't have an opportunity to offer her an alternative look into the future. Maybe that was how it was meant to be as

Kellie, my wife, couldn't get me out of there fast enough. So much so that she authorised an early pass for a beer if we could find a decent pub. I also couldn't wait to get the tie off that I had spent a good hour trying to fix around my trachi that morning.

Both of us agreed that it all seemed so negative and that people's lives were being written off before they had had a chance to start.

So, if anyone is reading this and has a youngster with an illness like Muscular Dystrophy, then I might just offer you an alternative viewpoint. One divorced from soft play and special schools.

My story is unique. I was lucky to have amazing people around me, but your child is unique too. I am not the American Dream, far from it, nor am I the benchmark. Furthermore, your child should not be pushed to be something that doesn't come naturally.

I am writing this to show you that there are other options.

I don't have all the answers, but I can at least show you I've had a bloody good shot at finding them.

Lee Evans.

STAND BY ME

It's a beautiful summer day in late July 2020 and the Garden of England is looking good today, fabulous even. The sun is scorching and I'm starting to burn up here, but somehow, I never learn. I'll sit here until I frazzle and then I'll moan all day tomorrow while I slap on Aftersun cream like it's a D.I.Y. emulsion job on a ceiling. You know what they say, "Mad Dogs and Englishmen" and all that. No, seriously, it is proper hot today so I move round to face the sun. We don't get many hot days in England so we have to make them count, don't we? But don't worry, I've got my floppy England cricket hat on and I feel like Michael Vaughan. I get all misty eyed and my mind wanders back to 2005 and the famous Ashes win. Put me in that hat and I'm invincible, I tell myself, I might even wear it for my next hospital stay.

As I dispatch my son Jude to get me a cold bottle of Becks out of the fridge, I shout out to Kellie, my wife, "What time are we firing that BBQ up, Babe as I'm Hank (Hank Marvin = starving) already?" Not only am I hungry, but I've pulled the trick of bringing another beer into play while we discuss food. You learn this skill early on in marriage, but to be fair to my wife she worries about me all the time, so a day of me drinking beers, with no water, on a scorching hot day, will send her into a panic.

Seriously though, I'm roasting here and I'm starting to feel like Ray Winstone's character Gary in Sexy Beast, "Bloody hell! I'm sweating in here. Roasting, boiling, baking".

That's me. So bloody hot.

Then I remember the cricket....... "Jude run in and look at the score; we're playing the West Indies son, so the screen will show W.I. Look at the score". Jude returns, "Daddy it's 43/3" and a loud cheer goes up from me. What a day eh?

The above story sounds like heaven; an English utopia of family love, sunny days with food, booze and a resurgent English cricket team chucked in. In reality it's a window of truth as the year is 2020 and the world is living through what seems like a plague; sad and worrying times due to the Covid-19 Pandemic. That afternoon gave us a rare return to our pre Covid-19 life. For a few hours we ignored the news, didn't watch the endless show of graphs from men in suits ("Next slide please") as we looked at each other in trepidation. What's the latest positive test number? How many deaths? The nation has had no choice but to become Grim Reapers and look for shreds of comfort in a decreasing number of 'Daily deaths in hospital settings from Covid-19'. And finally, the famous R (virus reproduction) rate, something that hardly any of us knew existed 6 months ago, but that is now of the utmost importance. A lower R rate, even by 0.1 would be a step towards our old life. But for today, just for a bit, we wanted to forget about how scared we were and still are, so we laughed, ate and tried to put all of our concerns to one side. God, it felt great.

It's been a time like no other. Nothing could prepare us for the change our world would experience. When I look back to late January and early February in 2020, it was clear something big was coming, but to some extent the world just pushed on as normal. If you avoided the news you could still say "Let's hope we don't get that Chinese Flu in the UK". I still went down the Den watching Millwall at the end of February that year, and as well, with my pal Chandler, I went to see Supergrass in concert in March at Alexander Palace. Then BOOM, the switch turned the UK off and life changed. I suppose the change began for different people on different days as they either reacted to news around the virus or twigged it was out of control.

My family started sitting up and listening in mid-March. A few trusted friends in the NHS had told us to be careful, very careful, around transmission of the virus as it causes chronic respiratory failure requiring 24-hour mechanical ventilation to enable patients to breathe. It is especially hazardous to those with numerous underlying health conditions, and as I also carry a bit of extra weight (I'm mid 40's now and it's allowed), I would be Covid-19's ideal blind date! Around this time I had a planned procedure at St Thomas' Hospital cancelled for a second time. I spoke to one of the nurses I knew at the Lane Fox Unit and she said it was already like a war zone there, so cancelling was the correct thing for me. Put simply, it wouldn't be safe for me to be in the hospital while Covid was raging within the population.

At that point Kellie and I made the decision to remove Jude from school and away from any possible virus transmission. We agreed to install the carers I have 24/7 in our small studio flat next door where they would be on standby. The logic behind this decision being that fewer people in the house, and then only when necessary, would create a safer environment for all of us.

So, the government made a decision to lock the country down and on 22 March 2020 the prime minister announced that Britain would be shutting down until the end of June.

The nation may well have been relieved to be able to "hide" at home from the virus, but I am told that the world outside became eerily quiet after that. Schools were closed, only necessary shops were open, only one person per family was allowed to shop at a time. A queuing system was introduced to make sure that shops were not crowded. Public transport was hugely reduced, flights worldwide were all but cancelled, and although offices were open, it wasn't long before many had to close due to the levels of staff infection and the concept of "work from home" became a "thing". With the benefit of hindsight, what did it achieve? For me personally, I came through that period, so I am grateful, but I can certainly see other people's frustration and anger.

We personally banned all friends and family from visiting us; basically everyone except my carers, and we began to live in our own very small world. We were still there a year later, just us three with a quick bit of help as and when needed from the carers.

So how was lockdown for us you ask? A nightmare! Nothing short of heart-breaking. From a practical point of view, my being a typical South East London man about town, staying at home for a year was always going to be a challenge. Most days I would be out doing something. I would often find myself saying to Kellie "Babes, I'm going to be back on the Manor tomorrow, so if you need something let me know," and off I'd go to London. I loved picking Jude up from school and popping into town, grabbing a sandwich from a cafe or a quick beer. At the weekend it would be something extra like a football match or a family trip out.

To then turn all that off like a switch, to say goodbye indefinitely to the life you know and love, felt surreal. As our lockdown commenced, I banged the table in Churchillian style and rattled out numerous home-made speeches of positivity to my kingdom which comprised of exactly two people, Kellie and Jude, and we quickly fell in to a routine. With the house locked down and entry limited to a select few carers, we actually felt a bit safer. Watching Netflix, eating junk food and being as one was great, and I still enjoy it to this day. The memories we've made as a family will last long beyond our lifespans and I hope Jude will pass these on to the next generation.

Does anything in our history resemble the past twelve months of disruption and the negative effect it had? Surely only the Blitz of World War II and the evacuation of London's children is greater. I can't think of anything else. With rolling 24-hour news, the sheer horror of what was unfolding across the world sent shivers down our spines. I remain convinced that we needed to know the progress of this "plague". The entire UK and the world needed that daily kick up the arse of "This is the shit we're in, this is how people are losing loved ones and this is how our brave NHS is protecting us." That's how I saw it. I'm a pretty black and white bloke who needs data and information. But the negativity was so overwhelming that it got to a point very quickly that we had to switch off from it.

My Achilles heel was Jude, our six-year-old son, missing school. I knew how concerned Kellie was about him initially missing out, and there wasn't any point in her trying to hide it, as it's a mother's prerogative to constantly worry about her child. When the schools closed altogether, however, Jude was in the same boat as everyone else. We threw everything we had into the home schooling and it proved to be our way of staying on track and staying focused. Luckily Jude is a diamond, a great boy and yeah, yeah, I'm his dad, so I will always say that, but honestly, he is! He's very grounded for such a young lad and so kind. Jude's school were also amazingly helpful by sending books and worksheets as well as by keeping in constant touch with us.

But, and there's always one of those, nothing could change the fact of how shit I felt. Nah, that doesn't do justice to how much of a disaster I felt. It was me messing up my boy's education. Yes, schools would eventually close, but in the middle of March it was me and my poxy Muscular Dystrophy that was affecting my son's education, interrupting this, the most important period of his life. Would this potentially damage this child that I love more than anything or anyone else on the planet? For the first time in my life, I hated Muscular Dystrophy. How mad is that? I didn't hate it when it killed my brother, we had both made a deal with big bad old M.D. by then; we had mastered it and how to stick 2 fingers up at it. I didn't ever hate it when I had been in hospital (almost 100 times now and still counting). Nah, when I'm in hospital I concentrate on what I'm going to do when I get out, something extraordinary; a treat, a splash of extraneous. Maybe a meal somewhere posh with the Mrs or a big day out with the chaps, just so I can say bollocks to you M.D. When I'm lying in that hospital bed having some horrible shit done, I focus on the reward I'm going to give myself. I imagine the Jack Nicholson character, the Joker, in Batman, and his famous saying, "Wait until they get a load of me". Once out, wait until I show old M.D. what I'm up to.

That's all very well on a personal level but sadly, Jude missing school found a weak spot in my daily battle with the condition. My guilt dragged me to tears, yet I had to push on and lead my family. They needed me. It took time to get my head around it and Kellie gave me some big talks, lots of understanding, and wise words. It's got better and Jude has actually done well. He is developing into a thoughtful, sensible, intelligent boy with a quest for a laugh and joke like any kid at that age.

Unfortunately, there will always be a part of me that struggles with having removed Jude from formal education. However, the slightly later complete closure of schools mitigated the issue somewhat. I do take some solace that this was a unique period in world history and one day people will look back at this first year of Covid-19 and say "Blimey, they've done very well; just a family trying to stick together and to look out for each other."

I spend a lot of time thinking about all the people who didn't get through this year and as a family we really do count our blessings. Seeing our great NHS step forward and try to protect the nation in a way an older relative does when a family is going through a difficult time has been humbling. At a time when we needed a hero, my own one who never lets me down just upped her game even more. Kellie has been unreal and a book could be written just about her own lockdown. For me the main issue is the disruption and worry for Kellie and Jude. For Kellie it was and is more complex; she had to factor in all my issues, including a 6-year-old son at home for over a year, and protect me without any of the support from relatives and friends we were used to. Her role demands commitment to our family, strength and decency, all of which she has in spades! Boy, am I in awe of her. She has kept this family afloat every day. Jude and I are both lucky to have her in our lives. Every day I make sure Jude knows this by pointing out the little things she does that would otherwise go unnoticed.

Jude himself has been unreal. He is so very protective of me and during lockdown he has taken charge of so much to help me. Getting the hoist ready to take me up, getting drinks from the fridge and any little errands that need doing around the house. It's easy to forget he's only 6. All this help has made my life not only possible, but considering the state of the world, quite pleasant! I certainly wouldn't survive without these two.

So I sit here with Ben E King's '*Stand By Me*' ringing in my ears.

∗∗∗

Right let's crack on about me. I started jotting down bits about my life years back, but lockdown has given me the time to have a go on the project of writing.

Let's make a start then...........

WE ARE FAMILY

So, when did all this start happening?

Let's start at the beginning................

I was born on 30th May 1975 at St Thomas' Hospital in London. My mum, Hazel, was a hard-working shop assistant, cleaner or working at whatever job she could find, and throughout my life she always seemed to be working. I can never remember my mum not working. She had an incredible desire to give us a decent standard of living as we were a working-class family and a hard day's graft was expected, my mum being the prime example. My dad, Dennis, had started out as a trainee butcher, then went into plumbing before becoming a scenery erector for the BBC or the Beeb as it was known then. Like my mum, my dad was a hard worker and would often do sixteen-hour days on the spin. The thing with Dennis was that he honestly believed everyone was entitled to a fiddle. In his eyes everyone was on the take and when I got a job in the Jobcentre, he was convinced I was nicking giros whereas my mum would have killed me if I was stupid enough to do that. Dad would have cashed them for me. He would tell you every butcher flogged nicked meat in the boozer and every copper takes back handers. It was the way of the world in his eyes, and he would turn up with wood, tools, clothes, you name it.

Remember those toys, Scooby Doos, where you made shapes out of two bits of plastic and wove them together? Well, Blue Peter ran a competition for viewers to send them in. At the time my dad was working on the show and he somehow obtained some that were not fit for display on the show. Why, I don't know. He then gave them to my brother Ginge and I to look through. We took them to school and our mates thought we were amazing. The best bit is that Ginge picked out a pukka one and sent it to Blue Peter for the competition. He only got a Blue Peter badge for it! I bet there is a bloke from Crewe still waiting for his badge and of course, my mum went bonkers when she found out.

My mum and my dad were so different. He was on strike once and money was really tight, so to make ends meet, he set up a stall on Westmoreland Road. His stall was the best and people were flocking to it like flies around shit. This was easy he thought, but word came down from other stall holders that two CID officers had started to walk down the market. Within two minutes 95% of Dad's stock was being scrambled into the back of the car and as my mum came back from the café with a bacon roll for him, I think she was greeted with around six items remaining to be sold.

One of my mum's best friends, Jackie, was a policewoman in her younger years. She is a lovely lady who went to primary school with my mum. She married a fellow police officer and then left the force to raise their family. Her husband, Andy, went on to become a high-ranking police officer. Once a year they would drive down from Hertfordshire to visit and as soon as my mum would say "Oh, Jackie and Andy are coming on Saturday", my dad would leap into action. Various tins of paint, boxes of nails and picture frames would be loaded into the car within minutes. "Coppers are never off duty, son," was his argument.

Again, my mum would go mad...

My brother Damien, or Ginge, or Dames, as he was known, was born three years after me and we moved about a bit in the early years with Kidbrooke and Peckham being home. We eventually moved to John Ruskin Street in Camberwell, to a tower block called Aberfeldy House and then finally to number 40, just further down in the same road where we remained for over forty years.

It was at Aberfeldy House that I first witnessed my dad's temper. One Sunday we were walking back from my Nanny Peg and Grandad Jock's place and my dad had been for a few beers with the in-laws. As we were walking to our flat, we passed a group of young lads sitting in the corridor and as my dad was carrying me, I was looking over his shoulder. I was about four years old and one of the lads threw a glass bottle which luckily smashed against the wall, but had sent fragments near to me and my eyes. My dad passed me over to my mum who was hysterical, and that was it. My dad was off after them and I remember how loud everything was. In those days everyone seemed to look out for each other more, and the neighbours had come out to help. People were trying to pull my dad away from the lad as he was seriously steaming into him. He can get a bad press and a lot of it he deserves, but in this case, he was protecting his family in an unprovoked attack and I can't imagine any father acting in any other way.

Having my Nanny Peg and Grandad Jock just two minutes' walk away was great. They lived on the Brandon Estate and were my mum's parents. For a young kid growing up, where they lived had everything (well, except a good chippy) from a good sweet shop, grass to play football on and a youth club. I spent my early years out back playing football with all the kids from the estate. I had already caught the Millwall bug and went through the years wanting to be the next Dean Neal or Steve Lovell. At that stage I had a decent first touch but I just couldn't seem to get any power in my shots, I didn't have the same acceleration that the other kids did and if I fell over it took me ages to get up. I wasn't fazed by any of this as the way I saw it was that Millwall had about eight shit players in the team, so these little difficulties shouldn't put a dampener on my footballing career.

But unbeknownst to me, a diagnosis had been made long before and the adults in my life were embarking on a battle they were unlikely to win, dealing with a life limiting condition.

Not long after my brother was born, my parents started to notice that something was not quite right with me. I had been walking for a while by age three, but I was also tripping or falling over unnecessarily. I walked on my toes a lot and couldn't manage to keep my heels on the ground, so my mum took me to our GP who put the whole thing down to new mum paranoia seeing as Damien had just been born. Nothing much happened after this and when I started primary school aged nearly five, we now had a new link via the school nurse. My mum mentioned her worries again. This time they were taken on board and a referral was made to the paediatricians at Guy's Hospital.

I remember going to the children's ward and after falling asleep with some sickly medicine, I seemed to wake up hours later with a big bandage around my left thigh. It was stinging and really hurting. The specialists had cut away a rectangular section of my thigh muscle to be sent off for a biopsy to give some indication

26

on why my mobility was so poor. As much as I was in pain, the presents from family and friends of Lego seemed to take the pain away as I was a massive Lego nut. I did wonder, if they did the same to my right leg, would I get the fire station given to me that I had been after for months?

After a few days I was sent home, not knowing it was a muscle biopsy and I doubt anyone in my family knew the impact these results would actually have. I still have that rectangular scar on my thigh to this day. Once I was sent home after my biopsy, I can't actually ever remember the results being discussed or a family conference about the diagnosis. In later life I found out that there was a huge family conference on both sides and it was discussed. Myself and Damien were just not part of it. You will tire of the mantra while reading this book; the stall was set out so Muscular Dystrophy would become part of our lives but not our life. All I can remember after that time was a lot of tears. There were no explanations or speeches, we just carried on and I can't begin to imagine what my mum and dad went through.

They had been told that I had Duchenne Muscular Dystrophy, a genetic disorder characterised by progressive muscle degeneration and weakness due to a lack of dystrophin that keeps muscle cells intact. The prognosis wasn't good with life expectancy being around age seventeen and no known treatments or cure. Today the life expectancy has risen to between age thirty to forty, but there is still no cure and this disease remains as direct and invasive as it was back then. It is estimated that around 2500 people are living with it today in the UK with around 100 boys born with it each year. There are many types of Muscular Dystrophy and Duchenne targets boys where there has been a genetic link. After long and extensive research, it was discovered that my mum was the genetic carrier which had been passed down from my great grandmother who was still alive at the time and was able to be tested. No one else in the extended family was affected by the gene, and maybe the most devastating blow was that my brother was also a confirmed case at a young age.

So, there it was; two boys, one condition and two parents falling apart. I expect my mum tried to stay strong and protect us, but then cried herself to sleep at night. My dad would have been in tears all the time and then on the missing list for a few days as he couldn't cope. None of us can really judge how they coped with it and for the purpose of this book I am not going to dwell on it. We didn't at the time, and I won't start now.

The stance of ignoring it all and getting me to tackle childhood as a normal kid was probably the most important thing to happen to both myself and my brother and I think my mum was the driving force behind it. This attitude carried on up into my adult life and put us both in good stead for life's challenges.

I was very young at diagnosis, my brother even younger, so there were no conversations like "you can't do this" or "you will never be able to do that"; it was more a case of "just be careful as your legs are a bit slower" or "slow down in case you fall". This reverberated throughout my entire circle of family and friends and that in turn made me feel just like anyone else. I had a very close network, and this started right at the top with my grandparents. As I have mentioned, Nanny Peg and Grandad Jock, or Walter if you want his real name, were a stone's throw away and provided so much help and support being so close.

Grandad was a proud Scotsman, or Scotch if you want to wind the jocks up, and from an early age I seemed to notice he hated everything about England. This would really annoy my nan. I mean if England were playing Germany, Grandad would support the krauts! As a young man I once asked him why he had not returned to Scotland and he would just blame my nan, saying she was settled here. I would laugh and remind him that he had spent the majority of his life down here. He was a hard worker and came from a small village called Ballingry in the Kingdom of Fife, working down the mines at age fourteen. I suppose anything London could offer him would have been a doddle compared to that and he had it hard as a youngster. I can't imagine what working in the mines could have been like for him. He was a man of morals and urged that you kept yourself to yourself and got on with life. The biggest crime as a kid was poking your head in the door of the Royal Standard pub while he was there, as it was off limits to kids always. As a man he was a giant to me, not only in height (six-foot one) but also in stature, and when my dad moved out years later, he became the biggest male influence in both myself and my brother's lives.

My Nanny Peg was one of the kindest people to have walked this earth. Of course, people say this all the time about family, but in this case it is true, and I cannot remember anyone saying a negative thing about her. She had an amazing understanding of life. She was an evacuee during World War II and was sent from Shepherds Bush out to Banbury in Oxfordshire. She would often call me "el Laddo", which would always make me smile, and in later years when I could be, well, a little hard work shall we say, my mum could be moaning to her on the telephone saying "Lee woke me up at 3am coming in with Jan and Jamie" to which my nan, who would always defend me and was my staunchest supporter, would reply with a "Well he's young, dear, that's el Laddo for you". Only problem was this would wind my mum up even more! Again, she was a hard worker who worked for the Civil Service as a typist. Their family home was such a happy place and a lot of memories from my childhood stay there.

On my dad's side I had my Grandad George and Nanny Grace. I thought Grandad George was just amazing. He served on HMS Belfast just near the end of World War II and would go around small islands trying to convince the natives that the war was over. He hated the Japs with a vengeance, and I remember as a kid him taking me to HMS Belfast to look at a bunk so he could point something out. In the metal was carved G.D.E., his initials for George David Evans and, wow, was I impressed. I could listen to his stories for hours and he was a good man, like Grandad Jock, someone you could look up to. I loved it when they would meet, as it was like two heads of state. "Jock", then "George", then two nods. The silence would break and then a call to the pub would follow, they were proper men, the real deal.

The final piece of the jigsaw is Nanny Grace. Now I am forever being told that I am mad, and if I am then these genes come from my nan, but all in a good way. She was one of the funniest people I have ever met and would either start or end a sentence calling me a little fucker. My nan had the ability to find a bargain, pick up a few bits and was wise to how this world worked. She wasn't going to be shafted and had no problem putting people straight when needed. Everything was straight forward as she had her game plan set out. I spent so much time with her growing up and the toughness she instilled in me has been priceless. She had a heart of gold and would spoil you rotten.

Growing up around these four people was a privilege, and all of them shaped myself and Dames in their own ways. Without them I doubt we would have got anywhere in this challenge to overcome the difficulties that had been chucked at us. You always felt loved and safe around them. You thought the impossible was possible and disability was never a word I ever heard one of them use, but I was very lucky to have straight talking family around me as a kid. While no one trampled on my dreams, they certainly didn't let me believe I could achieve anything unrealistic. Like a conversation I had at around 12 years of age with my Grandad George when I was showing an interest in aviation. I stated that I wanted to join the R.A.F. to train as an Air Traffic Controller which didn't end well. In a millisecond he cut across me and said "What a load of rubbish. The R.A.F. are not going to take on a bloke who can't walk. Concentrate on jobs you can do". To some this may sound harsh, but for me it was exactly the guidance I needed and still do.

Now I look at things in the same light. The physical hardware can't change, can it? I'll always be disabled and the sooner I came to terms with it, the easier life became. The software, though, can change over time. My feelings and emotions change yearly. I mean ten years ago I wouldn't have dreamed of writing this book and expressing myself, but look where I am now. All in all, I am part of a big family and I've always been pretty much the oldest cousin, certainly on my dad's side of the family. I think having the younger cousins coming into family life with a disabled member has been a positive for us all and we were supported by an army of aunts it seemed.

We had my Aunt Susan and Aunt Barb, both no-nonsense South-East London ladies who said it how it was, but would be there for you whenever you had any problems. My mum would always remind us that people like Susan and Barbara were there all the time. I also have two other aunts who played massive parts in my upbringing. Debbie, who is my dad's little sister and at only around eight years older than me, has been there from day one and still is today. When I think of times with my Aunt Debbie it was always happy memories and times that I cherish. These days I send Jude to stay with her so that he experiences those amazing childhood memories and he comes back spoilt rotten and absolutely loves it. Debs is still my go to person in times of trouble and really, she has taken on all of that problem solving and advice that my mum would have given me throughout my life.

My Aunt Diane, who is my mum's youngest sibling, seemed to be with us most days during our childhood. Only twelve years older, the age gap was also low, and while experiencing difficult times growing up, having her there was priceless. I will never forget how she supported us and took on those challenging times. Myself and Dames were so, so lucky to have Debbie and Diane there. Family units have changed but I still try so hard to recapture it for my own son Jude.

It would be impossible to mention all the family and friends who have looked out for us, as so many have shown us love and support. We have been blessed with good people around us from the start and Don was no exception. Growing up, my mum's youngest brother Don was around constantly during my early childhood years. He often came away on family holidays along with Aunt Debs and I absolutely loved these holidays. My dad and Don up drinking for England while on tour in Italy, Greece, Portugal and Morocco. He has a very good sense of humour and is a knowledgeable bloke, so these days meeting him for a beer or two is something I really enjoy and look forward to.

We were now settled in John Ruskin Street and I had just started at the primary school across the road called, funnily enough, John Ruskin Primary School. School was great, but I was one of those kids who just talks too much. I was never really naughty, but would always get told to keep quiet and concentrate. Unluckily for me, my mum was a cleaner at the school, so if she was cleaning and I had been a little silly in class, the teacher would have a chat with her. I would then be read the riot act by my mum and sent to bed once we got home. Things did seem a little unfair. I mean most kids would get met by their parents at the school gates. I was picked off like a sniper taking a hit and this may seem dramatic, but try explaining that to a seven-year-old.

I made some good friends at school. Big Marc, Hotdog, Frankie Fowler, Jan, Lee Fitzgerald, Ricky Page and some of these lads stayed friends for over thirty years. We were all football mad but me and Frankie were the only Millwall fans in the whole school, and it felt like we had been chosen. Both my dad and Frankie's dad were, shall we say, 'active' in the shenanigans at The Den. We would often return to school on a Monday with stories of what we had witnessed, and the effect it had on our classmates was that they wanted to go themselves, so we always took other kids with us. I like to think me and Frankie played a small part in Millwall's fan base growing.

One of the first struggles I encountered happened at about the age of six or seven. Getting changed for PE at infants' school was a nightmare. You would take all your clothes off, down to your underwear, and then go into the hall for weekly exercise. I would be using one hand to take the weight of my balance and then use the other hand to pull my trousers down, then I would change hands to swing round and do the other side. This was a time-consuming process, so I was allowed to join the class after the start of PE. A few times I would stumble or misjudge how far I had transferred from one side to the other, and the result would be me crashing to the floor. I will be honest and say that PE and getting changed was a nightmare due to my condition. The whole PE negativity was increased and the dressing issue was eclipsed on the day that, for some strange reason, I ran out into the hall starkers, in my full glory, only for all the kids to laugh and the teacher to scream "Get back and put your pants on!".

Nothing at all to do with Muscular Dystrophy, just me being an exhibitionist.

It was around the age of eight or nine that the difficulties of having this condition began to hit home and my understanding of it grew. As a kid, do you remember sitting cross legged in assemblies? When it was time to get back up and go to class, I didn't have the strength in my legs to push myself up off the floor. To get around this I would shuffle across the floor to find a table, then I would push my legs straight back while pushing my arms forward looking like I was about to do a push up. I would keep pushing my arms up and this would push my bum into the air. I must have looked like a sumo wrestler as I chucked my full body weight onto the table next to me. Once there I could push myself back and I would be rocking back and forth to steady myself and this is where it became difficult as I was swaying. I lost count of the number of times I misjudged it and ended up on my back after banging my head. The teachers then decided to put a chair at the end, next to the table, and it helped a bit, saving them from seeing the ungainly sight of my sumo impression. Like so many things around my disability I discovered that I could manoeuvre things to make situations work for me. This was to be so important to me in life.

While at John Ruskin Primary School I received an award which was reserved for a pupil in their final year. The Bob Cox Trophy was issued yearly, so it was quite coveted and it was awarded to a child who had overcome adversity. Come on, you know where this is going. In 1985 something unique happened at John Ruskin Junior and Infants School. They awarded it to a 3rd year (Year 5 in new money) child, me, and talk about ripping the rule book up. I have said many times during my adult life "Not giving a fuck since 1975" in reference to doing it my way and the Bob Cox winning moment was the first time I started to notice we were doing things a little differently. But to piss on my parade, my brother won it in his last year, not doing it with style, like me...He didn't care about my observations as they arranged for a Millwall player called Wesley Reid to give him the award.

Hospital appointments were starting to come more frequently and at the age of nine or ten that seemed brilliant, as it meant a day off school. We were put under the care of Hammersmith Hospital and it seemed like the other side of the world. The top dog was Professor Dubowitz and I think he was South African; I always remember that he was a really nice man. He would fly in from all over Europe to run a clinic and then go again. The consultant in charge was Dr Heckmack, and me and Ginge hated him. He looked like Tom Chance from the 80's sitcom 'Chance in a Million' and he had really wild hair. He seemed to love doing nasty tests. Blood tests were always wanted, and I remember him putting a large needle into my calf muscle. Some of you will think he was just doing his job and carrying out research, but I can tell you that me and Ginge didn't share this view. The thing is, we had started to work out this bloke's game plan. We knew if we sat down, that he had us captured, as we could never get up and out of the chairs fast enough. Well, they say "up there for thinking and down there for dancing", and in our case down there for running. We would just loiter around in the consulting room and when he started talking about blood tests one of us shouted "Run!" and we were off. For two lads with a muscle wasting condition, we couldn't half shift in this instance. My mum and dad would give chase with a few junior doctors, but once we were out of the room, we were gone.

Heckmack was a sly fox though and would position another doctor next to the door. How would we beat this? Either chuck something or one would run with the other falling to the floor, and if we did get out, we would split up. But it did get to the point where my mum wouldn't let us go through anymore rubbish. I suppose in the beginning she was taking us to the appointments in the hopes that it would help us, but once it started to distress us, my mum, being my mum, soon put the medical professionals straight. Around that time my mum made a conscious decision to take myself and Dames out of the firing line of tests and nasty procedures, as it was only causing pain and stress for us all. She still campaigned wholeheartedly to raise money for Muscular Dystrophy research and organised bike rides, sponsored walks or jumble sales. But she wasn't going to let me and Dames be used as some kind of guinea pigs and that's how we thought we were being used.

We were still under the Hammersmith and would still attend appointments with consultants every few months. We had some nasty tests done from time to time, but my mum had made it crystal clear that these would only be carried out if they were beneficial to our health. The journey to the hospital was a nightmare and even by car it would take nearly two hours, but the journey and nasty tests were often offset by a day off school and a McDonald's at Shepherd's Bush on the way home. We were receiving physiotherapy once a week and a physio would come to the house to do stretches on our legs and arms. It could be a bit of a bind as you would be just settling down to watch Jossie's Giants or Grange Hill and the physio would turn up for an hour's session. The scramble between me and Ginge to go first must have had the physio thinking that we enjoyed our sessions. What they didn't know was that I was already booked in to see Cally (my first crush) from Grange Hill at 5.30pm on BBC1. My mum was strict but fair, and you were under no illusions that you had to get on with it. We would leave the television on in the corner of the living room and if we did our exercises properly it would stay on but if we moaned my mum would walk over and just turn it off.

Aside from physio sessions, we had our regular assessment at Hammersmith. It was really tiring and would last a good two hours, which always ended with a 100 metre run down the main corridor. Whoever came up with this idea must have been on the wacky backy, as it was hard enough to run at the best of times, but even harder when dodging porters pushing beds, nurses on a coffee break and OAPs walking 2 mph. I lost count of the times me or Ginge went arse over tit!

Two of the funniest stories about us attending the hospital concerns two of the most decent fellas out there, my Uncle Shugs and Uncle Billy. The hospital contacted my mum saying the physios were carrying out a trial on a new technique and it involved sending electrical stimulus to your muscles. As this was something that may help, my mum believed it was worth a go. On the first day of the trial my Uncle Shugs said he would drive us over to Hammersmith (I think my dad was on one of his missing trips) and I always remember his car; it was a long black Austin 1800. I have never been into cars, but I loved this one as the speedometer fascinated me. I would be glued to it for the whole journey; it was a half-moon shape where the needle seemed to sweep like a Rolex.

Once we were there, the physios gave us a little chat on what to expect and how it could help our muscles. They said that the Soviet Union were using similar techniques to improve muscle strength in their athletes. Now I never got to the bottom of whether this was all bollocks to try to get us to sign up, but as it was during the Cold War, I was hooked on it. I think I even spiced it up to my mates by saying the Russian Cosmonauts and KGB were using it. After the pep talk, the physio wanted a volunteer to give it a go. As her eyes focused on poor old Shugs, you could see him thinking that he was only there as the driver. She explained that a small box clipped to your waist was connected to two pads on your calves and the settings were from one to nine, but for me and Ginge it would be used at around three to four. As she hooked Shugs up, it was ramped up to five and he was obviously getting little bursts into his calf that were quite uncomfortable, but being the decent bloke that he is, he didn't want to alarm his nephews. When they finally unplugged him from what must have felt like the National Grid, he was actually sweating buckets. We took the machines home and it wasn't considerable pain, just more like very strong pins and needles.

The other story I remember is Uncle Billy returning to my nan and grandads pissed as a fart and telling him about the machines. When male bravado kicked in, he instructed us to put one on his calf. Once Ginge turned it up to nine, Billy looked like he was in an electric chair in an American prison. When we got home, we told my mum and, of course, she went mad. My dad said we were stupid, but only because we didn't put it on Billy's cock. Two very different takes on parenting.

What happened to the trial? Nothing. Six months later they asked for the equipment to be returned, much to Shugs' and Billy's relief. Like so many things in our battle with finding a cure for Muscular Dystrophy, it never really got off the ground, although I still like to think that there are some KGB agents out there built like Arnold Schwarzenegger.

I had really started to work out that things were a little different for me and I suppose all the appointments, physio sessions and electric shock treatments got me thinking. I never actually believed that I was different to anyone else and I think that has followed through to the present day, but as I got older it did tone down a bit. My mum was always pushing me hard to live a normal life and I wanted to do all the things that other kids were doing at that age, one of them being able to join the local cub scouts. One Tuesday evening my mum and her friend Ceri took me to the church hall in Kennington but I was in and out in minutes, "Sorry love we don't have facilities for disabled kids". My mum's attitude was don't worry; we will get you into another one next week. So, the following week I was taken to the Camberwell Cubs. Once again, when she explained about my condition, it was a no-no and I couldn't quite understand what the problem was. Ok, I walked funny but that was it, Michael Barrymore walked funny and everyone accepted him, and I wasn't even in a wheelchair then. Like many times, as I would find out, it was other people who had the issues with my disability, not me. Again, my mum and Ceri said they would find somewhere else the following week, which would be Walworth Cubs on the Aylesbury Estate. So, the next Tuesday my mum went in to fill out the forms and said I would be coming in within minutes. Well I walked really funny, my back arched right back and I would walk on my tip toes. A feather could blow me over and everyone seemed to turn and look as I entered the hall, even Badger, the cub leader was looking (I was warned by my dad on the first trip to watch out for the bloke in charge as they are always suspect around kids; cheers for my innocence Dad!). After twenty minutes I was having the time of my life singing the National Anthem and preparing conkers to fight with, when an older lad asked if I needed the toilet. I said "no thanks" and carried on. After forty minutes a few lads were in conference in the corner and then called me over. I followed them and they led me to the toilet. We stood there in silence for thirty seconds and again, I was asked if I needed the toilet, again I said no. I started thinking that these lot were a bit weird and once back in the hall I re-joined the activities. When I saw Badger approaching and beckoning me to the toilet, I remembered what my dad had told me and made a bolt towards a group of boys occupied with a task. At the end of the night, when it was time to go home, my mum spoke to Badger. "He has loved it, Mrs Evans, but I think he needs to do a wee as he has been holding it in all night and walking funny". Once my mum explained my condition, he was fine. I attended there for a few years and made loads of friends as a result.

My mum repeated this sink or swim tactic many times. It worked when I joined Clubland and the Jack Hobbs club. It didn't work so well when I went to little league five a side in Kennington Park and the kids knew that all they had to do was touch me and I would fall over. I spent more time face down in the AstroTurf than I did with the ball, but on the whole, it worked. All the bumps and bruises were insignificant compared to the days out or snooker tournaments I played in and the friends I would make. I'm not sure the sink or swim tactic works for us all; it didn't work for my brother. Maybe it's down to personality, good judgement by the parents and most of all a huge slice of good luck.

BAGGY TROUSERS

So, I was now ready to make the move to secondary school and the years and friendships that followed throughout my teenage years had the second biggest influence on me, after my mum.

I started at William Penn, Billy Biro to those in the know, in September 1986. It had a very poor reputation, as its recruiting grounds were Peckham, Camberwell, Walworth and Brixton, with the odd posh kid from Dulwich chucked in (their parents must have hit hard times and couldn't afford Dulwich College). The school was set a few hundred yards from Dulwich Village and the village is still one of the most exclusive places in Britain. Over the years Margaret Thatcher, Mohammed Al Fayed and even Tom Cruise have resided there. Why they ever built a comprehensive school so near to so many rich, miserable and stuck-up people, only God knows.

Lunch times were always great scenes of amusement. Your normal run in with gobby kids went to a higher level, as the upper class took exception to Levi and Danny searching the village for a sausage roll. William Penn was a madhouse, a completely dysfunctional learning experiment. It should have been a casebook study of a failing inner city comprehensive educational setting, and both Mike Leigh and Shane Meadows would have produced a BAFTA award winning series if they had been aware of William Penn in the '80s. It had it all; out of control students paired with washed up teachers on the rocks who were drinking in the last chance saloon of the teaching profession, as well as at the Crown and Greyhound of a lunchtime.

The school setting was grey concrete buildings that wouldn't have looked out of place in the Soviet Union at the time. The place was falling apart and even had to endure portacabins when asbestos was found in the teaching block. Life at Penn was uncompromising and raw. Yet rising above all that negativity were an army of characters who you grew up with. Some you disliked, but a few become lifelong friends. There were a select few teachers who went above and beyond to push us on and support us. Mr McCann, my Geography teacher, and two disciplinarians, Mr McGlynn, a tough Lancastrian, and Mr Thomas, a West Indian fella, tried to install some self-control into us or hold some form of authority. . As kids we were shit scared of both of them, but in later life, we would appreciate the influence they had on us. Most importantly for me, it somehow worked as a secondary school and for this I will be forever grateful.

I had intended to go to Walworth but the lower school was in an old Victorian building and any form of adaption would be a nightmare. While at William Penn, Mr Hougham, the Headmaster, stated they would do everything possible to enable me to have a normal education, whatever normal is, and I still don't know, but even today it is something I strive to achieve, even though I know I will never reach it. As I have got older, I have actually noticed that I don't think anyone wants normality in their life. You start to go full circle and think normal is boring. Fuck normal.

On the day I started there wasn't one thing at the school that would have hinted that a disabled pupil attended. No ramps, doors that were no wider than anywhere else and a challenge to get through, and there certainly wasn't a disabled toilet. But what William Penn did have was honesty, a vision and a commitment to making the school accessible to me. That meant everything to myself and my mum, and I joined knowing that whilst the accessibility was pretty poor, they were committed to making me part of the school. It's surprising what you can achieve when everyone is rowing in the same direction.

Starting at William Penn was an achievement in itself. My mum had been told by the headmaster, Mr Comber, at my primary school, John Ruskin, that I would have to go to a 'special school'. My mum was very level headed and as much as she was desperate for me to go to a 'normal' school she would not let her wishes overpower what I wanted to do or the correct thing for me. Before we made our in-house choice, we visited the local special school, and as much as we were impressed with the cake making and soft play facilities, my mum's first question to the headmaster at the end of the tour was "When do they do their English and Maths?". Once he explained there was no option for this, he stated that after reading my last school report and meeting me, he didn't think a special school was the right place for me. After his verdict, myself and my mum adjourned to the Wimpy on the Walworth Road to discuss my education (I could get used to a day off school and Wimpy). I told her I didn't want to go there at all and wanted to go to a normal school with Big Marc, Danny Kidby and all the other boys. Whilst a special school wouldn't have worked for me, I still understand that for each individual with challenging situations, an individual decision that supports that child has to be reached. From experience, I know that some lads with Duchenne's found mainstream education a very difficult setting to develop in. One lad I went to school with had a very difficult time, and my brother didn't enjoy it as much as I did, and was your mid-range story of a physically disabled kid in a 'normal' school, but I could counter that with in these two cases it was their personalities more than their condition that affected their experiences. The lad I know had a bit of a chip on his shoulder, and my brother Ginge, well, as intelligent as he was, just didn't give a toss. He just didn't want to be there. If you're reading this and have a boy with Duchenne's, then my advice would certainly be to push him into mainstream school. I accept we are all different but the opportunity to learn and also build friendships has to be worth a punt. I accept that I may sound a bit patronising but I've done the whole Duchenne's kid, boy and man journey and I want to help and advise; that's the reason I've written this book.

As much as the first day was a challenge, we were cocooned in our own year block and an empty school outside to ease us into our new environment, but nothing could prepare me for day 2. The second day was when the entire school would return to join the protected species. The day they returned I would make a less than inconspicuous entrance into the school life. My walking was strange as I walked bow legged, back tilted right back and defying gravity (hang on, we've discussed this at my cub scout induction). The black lads had designed a not too dissimilar bowl to mine but just not as spastic looking. As I walked across the playground, I could feel the eyes on me, people were growling. A group of lads a lot older than me were shouting "Bad man, who the fuck does you think you are?" They started coming towards me and I didn't have a clue what the issue was. Luckily an older boy who could look after himself and was a young Roader, came over and explained that I had a condition, or as he put it, "a bit of a raspberry (Raspberry Ripple = Cripple). I got to know the lads that had taken exception to my unusual walk in later years at college, and we often laughed about my first meeting with them. The same day the teachers held an assembly without me. They explained my condition and how it affected me. It was no real drama, they just said he walks funny and falls over a lot. I was then left to get on with life and sink or swim like the rest, just how it should be.

Having a disability never made you exempt from piss taking, why ever should it? I am one of the biggest wind-up merchants in the world. I grew up with family and friends who constantly teased and wound each other up. School was no different, and the stuff we said then would get you expelled today and probably nicked, but back then teachers would laugh and some would even join in. Black kids were ridiculed about their afros, fat kids were reminded of their weight and many, many more that have been outlawed today. Me, I was a mong, spaz, and flid, every term that would send today's PC lefties over the edge. Do I think it's right to use those terms (about myself included)? Probably not, but in those days things just seemed so different. Nobody seemed to be offended and far too much pressure is placed on kids these days. We all grew out of it and you never sensed any real nastiness. Today you have 7-year-old kids being placed in the school's racism book. How the fuck does a 7-year-old know what racism is? By all means confront them and tell them it's wrong, but to put a black mark next to them at such a young age is just bonkers. The thing is, having the piss taken out of you didn't stop with the kids. I remember my class mates running to tell me that at P.E. they were running around the gym in a rather lethargic way and one of the games teachers yelled "Oi, faster, or I will get that cripple Lee down. Even he is quicker than you". No adults seemed to really take it onboard and when I told my mum, it was "Cheeky bastard. If he says it again tell him your dad will come down". This threat always seemed to work and I would mention this to friends as I knew it would work its way back to the vocal teacher. The teachers knew my dad was a Millwall fan and much to my mum's horror he attended my first parents' evening with a black eye (his excuse was he fell at work). The tactical call to arms to my dad was one I don't think I ever did use though, but I did use the threat once or twice when kids at school attempted to bully me.

During my second year (I think that is year 8 in new money), I was given a new challenge. The Hammersmith Hospital decided to make me wear callipers. To this day I am not sure if it was a trial or a medical breakthrough, but I would guess by the lack of kids using them today it was a trial that was pretty unsuccessful, and this calliper was a bastard to manage. You literally had to learn to walk again with the aid of physiotherapists. Trying to walk with these heavy plastic legs smothering your own legs was no mean feat. I will never forget how, if I mistimed my walk, my meat and 2 veg would get squashed between the callipers. Ouch. After learning how to attempt to walk with them I was discharged from hospital.

We didn't have a car at the time so my mum gave my dad instructions to borrow a car or even hire one as she would be at work and dad only worked around the corner at the BBC. When he arrived with one of his mates, Gary from Millwall, I was a little bit shocked at the form of transport. Gary was a window cleaner and they arrived in his New Century white van, where I was then dumped unceremoniously in the back for the drive home. After moaning about flying around in the back, (there were no seats, I was just laid out between the buckets and ladders), a pit stop was made to get me a McDonald's in what must have been an attempt to shut me up.

I was back at school soon with callipers and was allowed to wear a baggy pair of plain tracksuit bottoms. I talked my mum into getting me the new England tracksuit by Umbro, which was pretty much the dog's (the dog's bollocks) at the time. To be honest, the callipers didn't improve my walking at all, and if anything, I found them a lot harder to walk in and everything took twice as long. One plus point about them is that they had this little ridge at the top of your leg by the start of your bum cheek and if you managed to perfect the balance you could actually sit while standing. This took a while to master but was very impressive to an audience of 13-year-old school friends.

But unfortunately, I started to take this handy resting position for granted. While on a school journey to the Croft (or one of those educational big houses that seemed one down from Borstal) I totally made a fool of myself in a story that always makes my wife laugh. While there I struggled to use the toilet. Doing a gypsy's (Gypsy's Kiss = Piss) was a nightmare as I had to have enough room to hold myself up against the wall with one hand, while holding the tools of the trade with another. Before I could get into this position, I had to pull my tracksuit bottoms down without knocking the knee release that would send me crashing to the floor.

Why, oh why didn't I just ask for some help? But boys at that age are very shy and don't want people around when they are getting their tackle out, so I thought I would make as few toilet trips as possible. I had managed to avoid one for nearly 2 days and I was proper bursting. Rocking forwards and backwards trying to stop pissing all over myself and the school mini bus we were in. As we were driving through some country lanes in Sussex on our way to visit Battle, I knew I had to go. "STOPPPP SIR!". My cry brought the mini bus to a halt. I took what seemed a life time to get myself and the callipers out of the mini bus, but I told my teacher all was fine, just needed a wee. I maneuvered myself with great skill along the side of the bus. The tracksuit bottoms came down a bit easier than I expected and I didn't give a fuck who saw me, I just wanted that feeling of my bladder emptying. I put one hand on the mini bus window, looking to get comfy while I drenched rural Sussex with 2 days of piss as I adapted the calliper stance and sat back. For the first 15 seconds this was amazing, I hadn't had sex obviously at that age, but was sure this feeling was just as good. Then, to my horror, I could feel myself falling back. I knew straight away I was going backwards and with a large thud I landed in the irrigation ditch behind me, unable to move, with a large volume of piss shooting up in the air all over me. It was like a backward version of Del Boy falling in that bar in an episode of Only Fools and Horses. With the help of my teacher and school friends (the few not taking the piss out of me) I was helped up. The crazy thing is that in any other school you wouldn't be able to come back from a day like that, but at William Penn abuse was dished out at such a rate that they soon moved on to the next victims. At the moment it happened I did think how much I hated my condition and the situations it put me in and now I just laugh at that story.

Unsurprisingly the callipers were ditched pretty soon after that trip.

So, I was now around age 13/14 and just discovering the many things teenagers get up to. Walworth seemed like paradise (strangely I still love the place, but not as much as I did as a kid) as it had everything you could want. A Wimpy for a start. In fact, it had 2 until the one on Liverpool Grove became a Star Burger. With so many faces from your childhood around, you always felt safe and best of all everyone seemed to be a Millwall fan. Nowadays there is no Wimpy; the area has lost its community feel and even though we still have a decent Millwall following, Wooly Road has people walking up and down in Arsenal and Chelsea shirts. I have even seen a poxy West Ham one.

I seemed to spend all my time walking up and down the Walworth Road. Faraday Park and the famous Aylesbury Estate (once the biggest housing estate in Europe) were favourite areas to just hang about and you were always trying to get the eye of girls. I must have fallen in love two or three times a week. I would love to tell you I pulled loads, but it just didn't happen and I think the only bird I pulled was as a teenager with a girl on a family holiday to Cyprus. This romance seemed to be engineered by my Uncle Billy who was acting like one of those Asian elders. I think my dad clocked they had a bit of money and thought "invite them into our company each night in the hopes they picked up our extensive bar bill". So, as you can imagine that bit of a relationship was a non-starter.

After school I would still want to be with my mates though.

There were around seven or eight of us who were from Walworth and Camberwell. We would go to one of our houses and just do normal lads' stuff like football, computer games and joking around. Evenings, weekends and school holidays seemed to just cross over from our education. Even at a young age I try to encourage this for Jude, and I want him to bring his friends home. My pals have got me through some of my darkest times and most have been there since childhood.

Being a teenage Roader in the late 80's, like most boys of that era from my manor, my first sexual experience took place in George's Barber shop on Westmoreland Road. Thankfully this experience didn't involve George himself, who was a lovely old Cypriot bloke but not someone I wanted to get close to. But George's daughter Andriola was in her early 20's. She wasn't a stunner, but neither a state, and she had a cracking pair of Bristols (Bristol City's = Titties). As most young teenagers were a bit too small to need the full chair, she would take the headrest off, enabling your neck to get cushioned by her knockers. All my mates were talking about it so I was desperate to try it. On going into the shop, I gestured to George I was waiting for Andriola. Not put off by the 3 other young lads waiting, I sat in my wheelchair happily waiting my turn. Then I discovered how my disability could be a downer. George came over to inform me that my wheelchair wouldn't fit down to the back of the shop so HE would do my haircut at his station as you walk in. I was gutted and I had no choice but to accept this and get the double kick in the plums of a shit haircut from George with no tit massage from Andriola. I was disappointed for days, but wasn't prepared just to give up. I would return and walk over on my own next time I needed a haircut. So, with each day seeming like a year, I waited the 5 weeks or so until I next needed my Barnet (Barnet Fair = Hair) chopped. That day came and as I wheeled into the shop, I knew I had to get up and moving. I pushed and pulled myself up to a standing position and I stood for what seemed a lifetime to get myself ready for the walk to her chair. When she beckoned me over, I was walking like Douglas Bader in Reach for the Sky. My body was going in all directions but I defied gravity just to slump into that chair.

Was it worth it? You bet it was! Andriola's lungs all over my Gregory (Gregory Peck = Neck) was amazing. Remember the only knockers I had seen were Barbara Windsor's in a cheeky half covered flash in Carry on Doctor, so to feel these warm ones on my neck was brilliant. That for me was going to be my benchmark. Don't listen to others, never back down, put in the effort and you will get the reward. God loves a trier!

I'll always look back on my time at Penn and smile. Simply because it gave me the confidence and nerve to tackle so many problems in later life, and for me that's real education.

A SPOONFUL OF SUGAR

So, January 1990 would be the year I finally got my haystack (*haystack = back*) sorted. The pain was getting worse, my spine had really started to curve. If it wasn't sorted the spine would crush the internal organs of my heart and lungs. My trusty tin of Ralgex spray I carried with me had long stopped being the answer.

I remember my mum and dad taking to me a to a hospital appointment at Hammersmith Hospital on a cold Friday in December, 1989. There, an orthopaedic surgeon called Professor Bentley told us the ins and outs of the operation (around 12 hours, removing all the discs in my back, putting metal rods from my neck down my spine and into my hips and then returning the discs) and I could see my parents were in shock. He made it clear that it was an operation that needed to be done and very soon. Me, I have to be honest and say I was too preoccupied with the Italia '90 sticker book that had been released that day for the forthcoming World Cup. After the appointment we headed home. Millwall were away to Charlton the next day at Selhurst Park and my dad was going to take me as an early Christmas treat. The next day just as we were getting ready to go, our world was turned upside down. We had a telephone call to say my Grandad George had died on the way back to Kent. It was my first time dealing with losing someone close and a difficult period was about to become harder.

That Christmas is a blur really. My dad had done one of his numerous disappearing acts and by early January I was shitting bricks. On a cold Monday morning I was off to the Royal National Orthopaedic Hospital in Stanmore, North London. For a 14-year-old boy it might have well as been in Cambodia, as I didn't have a clue how to get there or where it was. The place was depressing enough; it didn't look like a hospital as it was an Army Camp when it was first built at the start of the 20th Century. It was made up of numerous little outbuildings which served as the wards. Turning up on a bitterly cold winter's Monday morning just added more negativity.

My mum had taken the day off work and this was going to be a nightmare for her. Working until 3pm then a bus to the Elephant, underground journey across London to Edgeware and then a bus to Stanmore. All while the family kept an eye on my brother. But she was tough, and if anyone was going to pull this off for her boy it was her. She must have been so scared as she had been told how dangerous the operation was. My Scoliosis (curvature of the spine) was severe. If it wasn't sorted soon it would start to affect my breathing. It had been made crystal clear to my mum what the implications were of not dealing with my problem. The Monday was taken up with speaking to the Consultant and his team. Professor Bentley, the Consultant carrying out the operation, was a nice man; old fashioned, very organised and to the point.

On the Tuesday my mum wouldn't be up until the night, so I was left to fend for myself. It was a real wake up call for me and probably went some way towards making me tough. First port of call was that they wanted get an idea of how much movement my spine had, so they could predict what would be a successful operation. Piece of piss, eh? Erm, nope. They strapped me to a chair, put this leather sex cap round my head, chin strap, everything. Then they used an old winch to start pulling me from my head. It was like a torture device but enabled them to have confidence they could straighten my spine. By now my spine would be around 35 degrees bent and the pain was immense. As a kid you don't normally take these things on board and I just wanted to get back to my Walkman and Stone Roses tape, but this time it was different. I was in tears and screaming through the pain.

The week went on with more and more tests, x-rays, scans, and measurements of every part of my body. On the Thursday night my mum came to stay and I was so pleased to see her. I had a long bath and was ready for bed by 10pm. That was the last day I ever walked. No one told me I would never walk again, it was just like any normal day. If I had known I wouldn't walk again, I think I might have done a bit more. Maybe a stroll to the end of the ward and back, but until I've written this, I never gave it much thought. Walking's overrated. The ability and option to walk was turned off like a switch, never to be available again.

The next morning, I was awake at 6am. A quick kiss from my mum and before I knew it, I was off on a trolley and knocked out. My last recollection was saying to a male theatre nurse "Look after me. I'm a Millwall fan and have loads of mates who will track you down". He laughed and before I could reply I was out. After 12 hours of surgery I had a blood transfusion and 2 Tungsten rods from the top of my back fused into my spine the whole way down and then crossed over and drilled into my hips, I was then complete.

But this was not the end. It was just the start.

I woke up 2 days later in Intensive Care, as high as a kite. Honestly, I was floating around the room. Just seeing my mum reassured me though, and I stayed there for 3 days before being moved back to the ward. I was told the operation had been a success and had gone to plan. Physio and slowly pushing on was the plan. Everything was going well until they took the catheter out. After about 9 hours I still hadn't passed any urine so I was told they would put another one in for the night and review it the next day. I'd never had one put in while awake before and the one I had taken out was put in obviously while I was under anaesthetic. Jesus, you could have heard me scream and shout in Timbuktu. A fella's Jap's eye is a sacred place. It's not meant to have a bit of plastic sticking out of it. Little did I know that I would go on to have easily over 300 catheters in my teenage years and 90% of them I would end up doing myself.

For the next couple of days, the cycle would continue. Take it out in the morning, sit around drinking all day but not pissing at all, then off into a side room at 10pm to have a new one put in. Life seemed pretty unfair at this point, but like Winston Churchill said "If you're going through hell, keep going". I just prayed and hoped for a better day the next day. Anyone who has spent a week or more in hospital will be familiar with this stupid question; "Have you opened your bowels recently?". It drives me mad. First of all, there are a million and one ways you can ask the question. Have you had a poo? Been to the toilet today? (It then becomes a 50/50 second question). Opened your bowels? It's like asking if you have opened the curtains this morning. Anyway, someone then worked out I hadn't been to the toilet for over a week, so they now had 2 things to work on. I had laxatives and enema fists. Well, it felt like it. I mean some old Tory MPs would have paid a fortune to have what I was going through.

My mum was up every day, but she had to work still to pay the bills. I was a kid in a hospital on my own and fucking scared. A young lad. Looking back, it was my grounding, my apprenticeship for future years. It made me understand many things even if I didn't know them at the time. But I was still crying out for someone to come in and fight in my corner on a daily basis. Every other kid had someone there when the doctors came around. Heroes come in many shapes and sizes; people say they don't always wear capes and that's true. Only mine marched into my life smoking 60 Embassy a day, putting people straight and combining the roles of Mother Theresa and Brick Top from Snatch.

On a freezing cold Monday morning my Nanny Grace arrived for an hour and stayed for 3 weeks. She was my very own Superhero and the reason I would eventually make it out of hospital. I had never been so pleased to see anyone in my life. The impression she made on the hospital and me was similar to when the Parachute Regiment landed on the Falklands to liberate the Islanders. She was on the ground and not taking any shit.

It didn't look like I was going anywhere fast and until I could solve the problem of having a wee, I was stuck there. I hadn't even had a dump for 3 weeks and my stomach was massive. I've been told I'm full of shit in my life, but this time I was. Just taking a bite to eat or a sip of a drink was painful, like I had been winded and kicked at the same time.

My nan was asking all the right questions, "Where is the Consultant who operated?" and "Get a specialist down here". Her questions weren't going down too well as these places don't like relatives getting too involved. I can see why, but for the poor patient who is stuck there they sometimes need that family member to be their voice.

As I've got older and had to speak up for family members, I've always gone for the polite but firm approach. My nan wasn't going to take that approach. Her grandson was in pain and wanted to go home. The hospital had made a balls up, but just wouldn't admit it on record. They talked about the dangers before the operation, and how just touching a nerve could cause irreversible damage, and they did seem to acknowledge something had gone wrong.

My nan had an affection for the C word, you know, Climbing Up Nut Trees. She was regularly using it and it wasn't going down too well. Nowadays she would have been banned for life, but there was some major piss taking and negligence going on, and I'm so grateful she was there.

Within a few days they had me booked in to visit a Spinal Injuries Ward and learn how to stick a catheter in myself. Funny that, as I had been asking for 2 weeks what the next step was and was told someone was looking into it. Nan had been there 3 days and boom. Was it coincidental or did they just not like being asked questions numerous times every day?

The Spinal Injuries place was horrific. Mainly young blokes who had come off motorbikes or builders who had fallen from roofs. They were able bodied blokes who had recently found out they will never walk again and they were probably still in shock. They weren't up for pep talks to a young lad and I didn't blame them. They spoke to me, let's say pretty clearly, about the lack of dignity of self-catheterising. They didn't mention the pain much, but bearing in mind the majority were paralyzed, it wasn't an issue. A nurse showing us around quickly moved us into a side room. My dad was quiet, but he was struggling as he was thinking the same as me. "What the fuck's happened here?" My mum was trying to steady the ship but couldn't either. We were all at sea.

Once we sat down and talked about how I would catheterise myself, it quickly dawned on me that it wasn't an option. Fuck that, I thought, I just can't do it. I'm not a quitter as a rule, but that was a bridge too far. We went back to the ward deflated, as I had built up learning to self-catheterise as my quick fix to getting out. My mum organised a meeting that day with my consultant. They were desperate to get me home; not only was I bed blocking, but they did want the best for me. To make it even harder, well, easier, if you pushed my stomach, I did my first number 2 in nearly a month. It was like a Boa Constrictor coming out, I think wars had been won faster than the time it took me to get this beast out. Once sorted the nurses returned with a Congratulations on your Birth card and I would have laughed, but my ribs were too sore.

At the meeting it was agreed that I would go home with a catheter in and the District Nurses would come out each evening to put a new one in and then take it out the next day. I was pleased really as I was not doing anything different to what I was doing now and had the bonus of being in my own home.

It would take some time to get everything set up and in place so I stayed in hospital for another week. In that time my nan was on watch to make sure everything was being done to get me home. She would hang around for the Ward Round, then stand by the nurses' office as they discussed patients. She would be asked to move on and she would remind them of the importance of contacting someone and her favourite trick was bumping into them in corridors and asking them questions. She even drunk in the Staff Social Club of an evening and she would pop down at about 9.30pm for a few glasses of Scotch. This was a double whammy for her; she could look to find someone from my ward to have a word with, and also have a nose to see which nurses and doctors were seeing each other.

They must have hated her, but like how the football world hated Sir Alex Ferguson; they all would love him to manage their club. She was my Fergie and I didn't give a fuck. She was my nan and was fighting in my corner; its what families are meant to do.

On a freezing cold Thursday evening in February, I was told I could go home. There was no hospital transport to take me and the likelihood was there wasn't going to be. I was stuck in Stanmore on the other side of London.

My dad came to bring me home, he telephoned my mum who said "Just get a taxi, we can get the money from my mum." Now Nanny Peg wasn't rich, far from it, but could always be relied on in an emergency. She wanted me home so much and had been holding the fort for my mum. Apparently, she chucked £100 At my mum and said "Get your boy home". That was a massive amount of wedge in those days, but good families stick together. As generations have gone on, we've lost that. Maybe because our grandparents lived through the War and experienced such hardship, they knew the value of family.

A taxi arrived after a few hours. It was disgusting really that they sent me home like that. A few weeks after major surgery and a catheter hanging out of me. A few weeks earlier the actor Gordon Kaye from 'Allo 'Allo had been in an accident when a tree fell on him. When he was released from hospital, he was sent home in an ambulance. If I had a penny for every time my nan reminded someone about how its "Ok to send a poor kid home in a taxi, but if he was a famous actor, he would get an ambulance" I could have bought my own brand-new ambulance.

We got everything in the taxi, it was piled high with clothes and medication. My nan was watching the meter like a hawk, and my dad was nervous but so happy to be getting me back to my mum. I felt every bump in the road on that trip, even though the hospital had me dosed up on painkillers for the journey. I didn't give a fuck, I was going home. I hadn't seen my brother in 7 weeks and I wanted to get home, get the Football Manager on, and get back to ramming each other in our wheelchairs while arguing about who were the better Millwall wingers; Jimmy Carter or Paul Stephenson. The journey took nearly 2 hours as the cabbie was trying to take it slow because of my back, but my nan was insistent that he was on a go slow to get the meter going. Once at home, I didn't even take notice of the balloons and banners welcoming me, I just wanted my bed to rest. Once on the bed my nan disappeared, but about 30 minutes later she returned with a large Lamb Shish and Chips from Walworth Kebab. My appetite had been poor all the time in hospital and I didn't eat a 1/3 of it, but enough to think I was getting back on track. It's no surprise if you take away the smell of shit and hospital bleach and the sight of someone being sick opposite you, you seem to eat a lot better!

Then, like Jonathan Smith in Highway to Heaven, Robert McCall in the Equalizer and the Littlest Hobo, you know all those great characters who come along and do good? Well, mine was my nan. She went back to living between Bermondsey and Folkestone and doing day trips on the cross-channel ferries to buy cheap cigarettes. Every time I saw her from then on, I thought of those dark days before she arrived. Once home and family and friends had gone home, the reality started to sink in. It was me, Ginge and my mum, all alone in our little council house. Being at home was brilliant. Just the things you to take for granted being on tap. Watching what you like on television, saying what you want and being as loud as you like, but most of all the normality of a normal life, well nearly normal.

Recovering from the actual spinal fusion was a doddle; lots of rest and relaxation. So, watching cricket and football, while lying on the bed with people bringing you take aways and sweets. The good recovery from the surgery was expected on release from hospital, but would only be a small part of my situation. I was still dependent on a catheter and I would have my dog, Luke, jumping all over me knocking the catheter stand flying. I would be sitting there from the minute I woke up, clock watching and counting the minutes down until the District Nurse arrived. They would come any time between 7pm - 11pm. Whatever time they came it was wrong as I just didn't want it to happen, but they were decent people and treated me well. I'd have my mates round playing Tracksuit Manager on the Amstrad and then would have to send them into the kitchen while I got on the bed to have it done. Most nights I would be screaming with the pain. The nurse would put KY Jelly on the catheter and every night I would forget to put it away before my pals returned, and every night the same joke about me and getting a bit of bum action would be cracked. My own fault as I should have learned, but maybe subconsciously I left it out for the joke to be aired as I needed something to make me laugh.

Urinary tract Infections were becoming an issue. I seemed to constantly have one. The Urologist decided that the way forward was to leave the catheter in all the time. What an improvement, I initially believed. No more pain through my bits, no nurses in every night. They would use a valve which would close the catheter off and I would then only use the catheter when I had the sensation to pee. This would keep my bladder working. This was all going great but while the UTIs were less frequent, when they did come, they were more severe. The catheter would often get blocked up which would result in a trip to A&E for it to be either flushed out or replaced.

One particularly bad infection around March 1990 came when the London Ambulance Service was on strike and the only way to get to hospital was in the back of a police van. When two coppers turned up, they didn't have a clue. I don't mean that badly as they were chucked in the deep end. They just wanted to get me to Guys Hospital as soon as possible. They lifted me and chucked me onto an old army stretcher and when they carried me out to the police van and opened the back doors, I half expected to see my dad in cuffs in the back after a long night out.

They laid me on the wooden bench and we were off.

These visits were every few weeks, but luckily it would be the ambulance staff who took me for future visits. It was a relief when they would say that flushing the catheter out had worked.

September came and I was ready to return to school. I was nine months behind my classmates with my GCSEs. One option was to go down a year and repeat the 4th year. That wasn't going to happen and I don't know any kid who would want to do that, so the plan was to work hard and try and come out with some semi-respectable grades, just enough to get into college.

It was disappointing as I was looking at A's and Bs before the operation, but I didn't want excuses though. I worked hard that last year. Don't get me wrong, I still managed to get in trouble with my teachers, but the progress I made to catch up lost ground was impressive.

It was hard though, sitting at a desk with a piss bag strapped to your leg.

I've always been a wind-up merchant. Gave it loads.

Growing up, nothing was off limits and I think the world was a lot easier. On the whole, boundaries set themselves. With a piss bag strapped to my leg I was an easy target, yet my class mates knew I was fighting to just get on. Not one kid took a liberty and gave me stick. I like to think it's a South London thing, well it was then, you stick together. Race, religion, disability whatever. When it mattered you looked out for each other. Sadly, it's not like that now.

A regime of constant antibiotics were prescribed in an attempt to keep the infections at bay. The tablets tasted vile, the most awful taste I have had in my life. I tried everything to disguise the taste and remove it from my palate. I can honestly say that Julie was wrong, a spoonful of sugar does not make the medicine go down.

I was still missing a few classes due to being poorly which meant unexpected hospital trips. Then, come January 1991, I was told that I have kidney stones and needed them removed.

I had been out of hospital coming up to a year.

So, come January I was taken into hospital again, just as the Iraq War was in full swing. I remember being told they had kept two wards empty on the top floor of Guys Tower in case of soldiers needing treatment. They hoped to blast the stones out, but if they couldn't they would cut them out. Obviously, this would have had an effect on my rehabilitation time. Luckily, they blasted them out and the doctor presented them to me in a plastic jar when I came around.

A few days later I was home and resting yet again.

Would the ride stop though!!

I was contacted by Guys saying that they felt self-catheterising was the way forward. Oh shit, here we go again. After speaking to my mum, she made a valid point that while it wasn't her who had to have it done, maybe this would break the cycle once and for all.

So, with more trepidation than a headmaster seeing Harvey Weinstein apply for the Drama Teacher's job, I set off on a bloody painful journey of learning how to self-catheterise.

I had just turned 15, and like any boy of that age I was thinking about my first bunk up. Honestly the motivation to learn was the thought that for twenty three hours a day I didn't have a bit of plastic in my cock. That's brutal honesty there. I wish I could say it worked and me and little Lee went off in the sunset to find the lucky lady to service it, but unfortunately, I had a few more years to wait.

So, I was booked in to see a nurse one morning who would show me how to use the catheter, where to put it, and to give me a talk.

Now my mum is squeamish, so she made sure she was in the kitchen doing cups of tea and well out of the way. When the nurse came, what do you think she was? My mates told me it would be a he and was gay and would still be showing me the workings four years later. Fuck off, I said. Nope. Honestly it was worse when she walked in. I would rather have had Dale Winton, God rest his soul, to show me.

She was a TOTAL TOP SORT. Yep, a right looker, fit as well. In today's money a cross between Kelly Brook with a touch of Michelle Keegan.

At first, I thought, "Brilliant!" But then, "Oh shit, how am I going to do this?" The first day was theory, the second day was practical. To this day, as she was showing me, I don't know how I managed to restrain myself and not poke her eye out.

Come on, I was a teenage boy.

But she was a lovely girl who just said, "Look this will get better. Maybe not today, but you will master this." By the end of the week, I had learnt to do it. It actually made life easier, but the pain was a fucker. I've said it before; I think expecting a teenage boy to do that was one of the few times I questioned life.

Within weeks I was catheterising at Millwall in those shitty dirty toilets at the back of the seats; had to do them at school, in the park. Even done one on a school trip to the Met Police's Hendon Training Centre - only fair really, after the number of times they've taken the piss. But I did it. Somehow, I made it work.

William Penn had a poor reputation, but the staff did everything they could to help me catch up. Mr McCann, my geography teacher would give up lunch breaks and free periods to tutor me. I ended up with a respectable C grade. Brilliant really, as I was doing 3-day weeks for a large period and had a misty academic year the year before. I came out with a few more C's and the rest were E's and D's. Nowhere near to what I should have achieved, but a great accomplishment anyway. It taught me something I never understood; how strong I actually was and still can be.

I learnt pretty quickly the attributes of resilience, determination and tenacity. I never knew I had these in me. It was my battle with Muscular Dystrophy that gave me access to these priceless gifts.

My grandad Jock had been down the mines. He never really showed any emotion. But when the GCSE results came through, he put his arm around me, hugged me and said "The great man Winston Churchill said 'Never ever, ever give up'. You didn't and you got your reward, don't ever forget that."

YOUNG GUNS

Everyone has a decade that defines them. Uncles will go on about the swinging 60's, my dad loved the whole lawless thing of Millwall in the 70's, but for me it has to be the 90's. It had it all; a war to start us off with, great football with the England team of Italia 90, great music, Millwall getting to Wembley, my own discovery of booze, drugs and birds (all in minimal amounts and never as much as I liked), and the passage from education through to grafting and earning a bit of cash.

These were great times and I always look back on them with a smile, but there were down times too, with the operation on my spine, my mum and dad getting divorced and some pitiful Millwall teams. It was now that my disability really kicked in.

I had just recovered from the spinal fusion and I was at home recovering for most of 1990. By 1991 I had improved, but still suffered from severe pain in my back and I had recurring kidney infections. I had to perform self-catheterising twice a day and sometimes the hospital would leave one in for a few weeks.

We've been through all of this already. I've told you all of this crap about my health.

C'mon, you know the apple about my situation and being ill.

I had an eye for the birds like any 16-year-old, but how would it work for me? A date in the Wimpy with me having to go and stick a tube in my Hampton wasn't top of many girl's lists of first dates was it? What about if she actually fancied me and I was going to get a bit of slap and tickle? How could I say no because I have a tube hanging out of there?

So, by no plan or thought I just fell into the world of admiring them from afar.

It wasn't just the birds. I was trying to grow my hair into a ponytail. Now I often say my mantra in life has been "turning a negative into a positive", well, with hindsight this is so true. My ponytail attempt was shocking. I wanted to grow it long like Ian Brown of the Stone Roses, and then tie it back into a ponytail most of the time. Unfortunately, the headrest on my wheelchair just squashed the very small ponytail I had, and gave me a scruffy look like I hadn't combed my hair. Not to be defeated, I went against the advice of my family and friends and went for a ponytail coming up from near the crown on the top of my head. It was totally stupid, and to a put a final nail in the coffin, a group called Deee-lite released a song called 'Groove is in the Heart'. In the video, one of the band members has a stupid silly ponytail like mine, so after lots of abuse, it went over night.

Apart from the complications with my spinal surgery, being in the wheelchair didn't affect me too much more. I had some good friends; the Walworth Road was the centre of our world and the fortnightly trip to the Den was our get-away.

Obviously as I got older, I noticed things more about the wheelchair and the barriers it would put up. In my late teens mates would discover lads' holidays to Ibiza but this was a non-starter for me. It did seem a little harsh, but I just thought well, maybe they get to shag Suzy from Skegness; well, I will get out and find Becky from Bermondsey (albeit a larger, more experienced version).

After working hard to finish my GCSE's and catching up on time missed, I managed to leave with some good grades, so the next step was college. I wanted to study science and to this day I don't know why I chose it. It was a subject I enjoyed, but had to really work hard to get good grades in, whereas geography was a total waltz for me. I enjoyed it and found it easy. My old geography teacher, Mr McCann, was a great teacher and always pushed me on. I wanted to experience a different location to study. I needed to get out of the Walworth Road. Some people go up north, others even move abroad. Me, I went to Putney. Yep, bloody Putney. It was only 11 miles down the road but it seemed like a different world. I would get up and talk about "My journey to Putney" like it was a horrific commute.

Everyone seemed so sophisticated in Putney and I loved it. The reality is that it's just a nice suburb of London really.

I worked hard at college and gained a B Tec National in Science which was a respected qualification at the time. Before I could even blink, half of the 90s had passed. I was now working in the local Jobcentre and had an income. This opened so many doors socially. Money gave me the opportunity to indulge myself and clothes become my first real extravagance. Growing up we always had nice clothes and my mum would do overtime at work to enable her to get us new trainers or a shirt for a family occasion we had to attend.

From around twelve or thirteen, if myself or Ginge received money as a gift for our birthdays, we would buy a nice Lacoste shirt, so we already had an eye on the clothes we liked. As a family though, we just didn't have the money to be constantly wearing the clothes we wanted as young-uns. That changed once I started working. Ginge and I would regularly have a trip up the West End to get some new bits of clothing. I would always give him some cash to treat himself. As brothers our bond was dynamic, loving and unique. We both looked out for each other and wanted the best in life for us both.

Going to football had a massive influence on my choice of clothes; the casual scene was in full swing, so I would often look at some of the lads at Millwall before I started working, and think, first pay day I get as a grown man I'm getting a pair of those Armani jeans that I noticed someone wearing. Being part of a group, a tribe, a following, a culture, whatever you want to call it, gave me the strength to push on without even knowing it. I wanted to be one of the boys and have a Henri-Lloyd jacket, and I quickly realised I needed to work.

Once working I'd be going away days with my Stone Island jacket, Ralph Lauren shirt and a nice Lacoste jumper. Nights out would be Gucci loafers or, my favourite at the time, Wannabe by Patrick Cox and a nice pair of Armani trousers or a decent pair of Jeans. People will laugh at how we followed the train, and I accept that, but for me I was just another lad; so was Ginge, and it was a major factor in what enabled both of us to succeed in living a normal life.

More years passed, we loved our music and Ginge was the conductor on this. He knew so much about the music we all loved. Britpop was our soundtrack. Yet, during all these years of happiness and making memories that would last a lifetime, I still struggled to pull a bird. Years later I can say that I more than made up for it. Like London buses, I had a period just before I met Kellie where it all clicked, but at one of the most crucial periods in my life it just wasn't happening. Apart from the odd date and one or two drunken kisses, not much happened and I questioned so much about myself. I would sit in pubs and watch total twats act the idiot all night, blokes who weren't the best looking, lads who would be rude and showing off in front of their pals. All of these would walk out with a girl at the end of the night. I never once talked about the frustration and upset to anyone. I was embarrassed and knew there was nothing anyone could do. I never even told my closest friends, so I bottled it up and pushed on for more. I promised myself that one day my time would come and I would get the same attention as everyone else. It all came true and I went on to meet many lovely girls. Best of all it came good in my early 30's when I met Kellie. If I knew about Kellie at 19, and I knew one day that she would be mine, I would have happily waited. She's that much of an amazing person.

But i didn't know that, or even know Kellie at 19.

I was a young lad who fancied anything that moved, but luckily most of my mates were nearly as poor as me in the pulling factor. I knew the reason behind my lack of success was the wheelchair. I was trying to attract girls between 18 – 25, but let's be sensible, they were just not interested. The ones who did seem to be at ease with my disability just wanted to be friends. So the 90's have flashed by and I can count my conquests on three fingers. A whole decade of success.

The next decade in the Millennium would be a 50/50 split o. happiness and severe heartbreak. I would succeed with the opposite sex, friendships would be stronger than ever with the boys, and I would achieve so much. Then I'd be tested by the deterioration in my condition and broken by the loss of my brother who I worshipped.

You'll find all that out, but the 90's are over and I will always look back and smile.

LET 'EM COME

***

Well, this bit is something I have really looked forward to, football, and more importantly, Millwall. I've spent so much time and money following Millwall, with so many ups and downs and that rollercoaster journey reflects my life pretty much. Going as a kid with my dad, the walk from parking the car in New Cross to The Old Den seemed like a marathon. My tired and weak legs nearly giving way but I was always pushing on as I didn't want to give my dad an excuse not to take me again. Being left outside the Duke of Albany if we were running late. I never grasped the logic until I started drinking myself. He would say "We aren't going to the Canterbury as we are running late, we will go to the Albany," and the end result was we always missed the first 5 minutes anyway, so I didn't get the logic.

Walking into The Den always made me nervous as a kid. You always knew something could happen and it was that sense of the unexpected, and then waiting for it to happen, which made me nervous. The attendances at games in my childhood were very poor, yet for a small lad it seemed the entire world was present; the noise and roar of the crowd was unique to this special corner of South East London.

I have made no secret of the fact that my dad was very active in being part of Millwall's bad reputation and while it's not something I would be in a rush to tell employers or future in-laws, neither is it something I have been ashamed off. Dad liked a beer and got into fights. He wasn't a terrorist or child killer, but just someone who, like many others, seemed to find himself in punch ups rather easily on a Saturday afternoon. Let's not forget that this is the 1980's and the working-class world that people like my father lived in was totally different to today's entitled society.

I have always laughed at how the media and the Government make football lads out to be people with no interest in football. You couldn't be more wrong if you tried. They love their clubs, and are normally there when the clubs are going through the shit times. They will be around supporting their team when the middle-class prawn sandwich eating mob have got bored and returned to rugby, the theatre and putting the world to rights. Also, continuing with the bad press, I haven't ever seen any hooligans I know start on innocent people. It is normally your wannabes who start on families and people in football shirts, and the actual chaps are just looking for like-minded people.

Let's be clear here. I'm not defending moronic idiots who tarnish the reputation of football with racism and the "chav" behaviour of indiscriminately chucking bottles and coins. The group I'm defending are football casuals. An example of this is disabled fans. I went to Plymouth in about 1996 with two mates. We ended up walking into a random pub full of their boys. They knew we were Millwall and treated us well. They knew what time Millwall's boys would be about and didn't see the point of picking on a bloke in a wheelchair with his two mates. That's how it should be and ALL proper Millwall I know would never take a liberty with a disabled fan. Of course, there are idiots who try to jump on the bandwagon, but thankfully they are normally put in their place. I personally have experienced the wallies of other teams trying to take a liberty, as a lot of disabled seating areas are in the home fans' section. This can obviously cause issues if someone takes offence when you cheer and most of my horror stories regarding this occurred when I was younger.

At Stoke's old Victoria Ground, I was sitting in the Stoke fans' end for the first game of the season. Amongst all the red shirts was me and my mate Tippler in blue Millwall shirts, and it was the only time I have ever worn a Millwall shirt to a game. During the game, which we won through a rare goal from that septic (septic tank = yank) international hotshot, Bruce Murray (great perm), I was pelted with chips and beer, and spat at. After the game I was offered out by spotty tramps in Kappa tracksuits, and I always love the weedy bloke who goes "you're lucky you are in a wheelchair, mate, or I would do you". Yes, my friend we are both lucky as I'm 6ft 1" and would smash you to pieces, I guess. But, as I said, I guess that makes us both lucky. I got speaking to some Stoke lads from their firm, the Naughty40, at a concert a few years after, and they were embarrassed when I was telling them. Same happened at Roots Hall in the early 90's. I had gone on the Saturday with big Tippler, but the game was postponed. When we went back for the rearranged game on the Tuesday week, it looked like half of South East London were there and had been drinking since the original game! We met my dad in the Railway Tavern in Prittlewell. He was the worse for wear and tagged along with us to the Southend stand to sit with me. Stan Collymore was playing for them, and from that day I have always detested the bloke. By the time Collymore had scored and the Millwall fans began to riot, we had been noticed as Millwall fans. The second-hand car dealers and spivs around us didn't really

78

seem that bothered, but as I was watching the game a group of youths aged about 18 congregated behind me. As I was at the back of the stand, I didn't take much notice as one gave me a push and chucked my Millwall baseball cap on the floor. It was bullying of the highest order, I was minding my own business, was with two others and I was in a wheelchair. Within seconds my dad had jumped over the seats, chinned the first one and was on his way for the rest of them. Sadly, his defence was now turning into an offensive and he was being watched by the Essex Constabulary who seemed to have had him on the floor just as quick as he had vaulted the seats. He was marched outside with us in pursuit. We pleaded for him to be released, but it was falling on deaf ears, and just as he was being carted away a steward came over and said he had witnessed the blokes starting on me. To our surprise they let him go, but I think the trouble in the Millwall end meant they were of more use there. With instructions to go straight to the train station, we did what a normal (that word again) Millwall fan would do, went to find a pub that was open.

Back to my dad, Gentle Den as he was known at The Den, or the Duke to us youngsters. I loved our trips to The Old Den but by about the age of nine I could always work out if I would be going by just looking at the opposition. If we had Portsmouth or Swansea, then I just knew it was a nonstarter for me. Oxford or, say, Exeter meant I probably would be taken but would be on standby to be perched on a wall if something escalated. Of course, Wimbledon or Bury at home would be a definite yes. My mum never really knew what it was like as my dad always

79

drummed into us that what happens at football stays there or you won't be going again.

The Old Den under floodlights was one of the wonders of the world for me. The ground was massive. The half way line terrace was like another continent and I never managed to make that journey over there. Our home was the floodlight pylon on the left of the Cold Blow Lane stand. My dad would carry me up the stairs and lift me to the edge of the pylon wall to sit on it, and it was like sitting on the top of the world. We had some good times there as kids. Myself and my brother would sometimes meet up with our mates Jodie and Jamie Kempster, and we would muck about as their dad Dedge and my dad would be holding court with their friends and the game would be a sub plot.

It wasn't really until our promotion season in 1987/88 that the obsession really kicked in. Up until then I was happy going as and when my dad decided, and I was happy dreaming of being Steve Lovell in the playground at school. In 1987 we really seemed to go for it. John Docherty had bought in George Lawrence, Tony Cascarino and a few others. In all my lifetime Millwall have always been as tight as two coats of paint. My dad says it has always been the same and he will always follow it up with the time we could have signed Kevin Keegan for £5000 from Scunthorpe. I always believed it was an urban myth as it sits well with the thinking of Millwall being tight and with Keegan being my favourite non-Millwall player, I met him a few years back and he confirmed it was true.

So, when in '87 they seemed to have a punt on promotion, everyone seemed in shock. That was a great team we had, our finest. They certainly epitomised the Millwall spirit as you had Hurlock, Briley, Cascarino, McLeary, Sheringham and a favourite in Danis Salman. Now these boys were tough, even Teddy when they had to be, but they could play too. That season Cascarino took my football heart away from me and even to this day he is still my all-time favourite Millwall player. Better, more skilful players than him have come and gone, like Alex Rae, Colin Cooper or Tim Cahill, who have all been better players, but for me Cas was the man. I was 12 years old and fascinated by how high he got up in the air and won so many headers and scored so many goals.

At the time, a lovely lady called Jayne Watson was employed to look after me at school. Every day I would go on about Cas and in the end, she wrote to Millwall who arranged for me to meet him. It's still one of my happiest childhood memories. She took me to The Den on a Tuesday afternoon (the school even let me have the day off), bought me a can of Coke and took me to the player's bar. I sat there for an hour asking him so many questions. A few years back, aged thirty-eight, I went to a Legend's Day at Millwall, and all the promotion squad were there. It was still only Cas that mattered. I sent my mate over to bring him to our table (I ain't a Mafia Don, it was just too packed to get my wheelchair through). As he walked over, I went "It's Cas, and he's coming to speak to me". My wife started laughing and said, "Pull yourself together you prat". Was she right? Probably. But that's football for you, and over thirty-five years later I still think he is the greatest; even if he has chucked our fans under the bus a few times when the media are baying for our blood.

I remember us playing Stoke at home a week before promotion, and I was desperate to go to the game. My dad had done one of his Lord Lucan's, a proper disappearing act. He would do them quite often as we got older, and I think it was partly because he couldn't handle the situation with myself and my brother Ginge's condition, but also his desire to get away and have a beer did have some bearing. The first time he went was truly awful. Me and Ginge must have been 12 and 9. He just went one morning and didn't come back. It was horrendous for my mum, nan and grandad as this was before mobile telephones and social media, so if you didn't want to be found it was easy. The police weren't interested as there were no suspicious circumstances, and he was a grown man. Everyone tried to protect me and Ginge from all of it by saying he was working away, but we soon twigged.

Anyway, by the morning of the Stoke game he had still not returned and was now five days AWOL. People were worrying as they expected him to come home by Friday, sod the family, Millwall had a big game. On Saturday morning my nan was in overdrive when we went shopping as she said we need to go and look round my dad's old Millwall haunts and ask his pals if they had seen him. Blimey Nan! He could be in any of 50 pubs within a 3-mile radius of The Den. We started down The Blue. My Nan was a real tough character, and she was ready to put his mates straight if they defended him. She was an old Bermondsey girl and going into a pub to confront a few Millwall boys would be no issue at all. After a few hours, there still was no sign. It was getting nearer to 2.30pm and we were getting closer to The Den. I started guiding my nan towards Millwall as the pull of the fans and excitement was too strong. "Nan, I reckon he will go to the match".

We got to the ground just after kick off and my old nan got me and my wheelchair up to the back of the Cold Blow stand. Stoke City had some good players and I think Steve Bould and Lee Dixon played that day. While I watched Teddy score in a 2-0 win, my nan scanned the terraces like a police spotter but still no sign of dad.

On the walk home, while I was honestly upset and worried that we hadn't found Dad, I still had so much excitement about us on the verge of promotion so chucked in the customary saveloy and chips; my mood was still magic.

Oh, dad did return a few days later. He walked into town to face a bollocking from his father, my Grandad George. To this day it is still one of the best Fergie style 'hairdryers' I have ever seen.

Dad went onto these 'missing lists' a few times over the years. Others were quick to judge him and yes, he was wrong to do it, but I can understand why he did. The situation with myself and Ginge was just one big pressure cooker. Dad just simply couldn't cope and it doesn't make him a bad bloke in my book. Don't judge a man until blah blah, you know the rest, but it's true. But like so many dads from the 80's onwards, their own needs came first. While I get the whole struggling to cope with a situation, my mum didn't have the same luxury of walking away. In my case it has to be a situation where I understand the whole equation of my dad disappearing, otherwise I would fester resentment and would never have anything to do with him. He made his choice to move on and enjoy the single man's life, then find a new family. I don't have an issue with that, even though it was heart-breaking at the time. For me it has to be clear cut what he couldn't cope with and what he chose to do out of choice. I don't know how, but somehow, we have managed to keep that crucial bond alive.

I suppose for a 12-year-old boy I probably didn't comprehend the significance of Millwall making it to the top flight. My dad, Uncle Billy and all the older family friends certainly did. I remember being at my nan and grandad's in Bermondsey the day we beat Hull to celebrate promotion. It seemed to be a non-stop party everywhere you went, and I would have loved to have been 10 years older and out with the chaps celebrating.

The final game of the season was against Blackburn Rovers at home. We would be getting the championship trophy but, on the day, we were thumped 4-1 but who gave a monkey's (toss)? We were up. No one wanted us there, but we had done it. I remember my dad taking me to the Canterbury Arms at 9am and it was packed. I was desperate to get to the ground early but everyone else just wanted to get pissed and I finally talked my dad into leaving at 2 o'clock. We still stopped at an off licence for beers on the Old Kent Road though, and while I was outside a young bird in her 20's ran up and gave me a big kiss, then pulled my head into her Bristol's (Bristol City's = titties) and ran off. Did I look older? Was she into young lads? Was she pissed and just in the party mood? We will never know, but sadly for my dad and his pals she was long gone by the time they rushed out of the shop.

One final pit stop for saveloy and chips and we were off to The Den. Blimey, Millwall promoted, birds sticking tits in your face and saveloy and chips. The world just seemed perfect that day.

Now, disabled facilities today are on a different planet to the 80's. At Millwall I was positioned next to the tunnel by the window of the laundry room, and my range of view was about 15% of the pitch. Did I care? No. I was at the game, I could hear the crowd and my heroes were in front of me. For this game I had Steve Archibald and Ossie Ardiles standing next to me. Millwall are my love, but I do appreciate football in general, and I was in awe of seeing them. Also, my dad has some strange habits. Both myself and my brother Ginge loved the film 'Escape to Victory' and that season my dad suggested we took the cover and ask Kevin O'Callaghan to sign it. We did this, and every game we went to, he instructed us to take it in case we saw another player from the film. After doing it a few times we got bored and stopped taking it, but he would do his nut.

But on this day for some bizarre reason, I had taken it. Luckily for me we managed to get Ossie to sign it (we also have Russell Osman from when he was the Bristol City Manager and John Walk from when he played for Middlesbrough at The Den). The biggest bonus of being in the wheelchair at The Old Den is that you had to walk past the dressing rooms to get out. So, as we left the ground and walked past the dressing rooms, we saw Les Briley jumping around with a bottle of champagne. He called us in. I remember my dad taking a big swig of it and all the players were going mental. For a young kid from Walworth who was Millwall mad, this took life to a different world.

It annoys me when people say disabled people use their disability to their advantage. As I say, "Why fucking not?".

I honestly don't think I do, but what I do though is make the best of a bad situation. Look, I would have loved to have stood on the terraces of the Cold Blow Lane stand with my mates that day, but I couldn't. I would have loved to have had a 100% view of the pitch, but I didn't, so, I got a little touch that day and I bet my mates would have swapped places with me. But would they have done it the other nine times out of ten? Of course not. Sadly, we live in a society of jealous people who love to moan. That day still feels like a dream, even all these years later.

The top flight was nothing like today's Premiership. Every team excited me so much more than today's clubs. Maybe being a kid had something to do with it, but even the lesser teams like Coventry and Southampton all had something to look forward to. Our first game at Villa saw a familiar occurrence, my dad going off with his mates and leaving myself and Ginge behind. I would have done anything to be there that day, but it was not meant to be. One thing that missing out on all these away games did do for me. was give me the desire to push on and stand on my own two feet in later life. It made me desperate to get to away games once I was older, and I more than made up for it. Sometimes you can have too much too young, and I took loads of my younger cousins all over the country as kids. They saw Millwall at Old Trafford, in cup finals at Wembley and the Millennium Stadium and all it did was burn up their hunger. It some ways they had it too good too soon. For me, my two away games in the top flight probably did me one of my biggest favours in life, Wimbledon away at Plough Lane, two seasons on the spin.

It was at a young age that I encountered my first football heartbreak and supporting Millwall would ensure many more, but this was my first. It happened at about age thirteen. Up until then I presumed that all footballers took football to be the beginning and end of life, that they gave 120%, 24 hours a day and if they lost a game, they would be on suicide watch for the next few days. Just a few months before the heartbreak happened, I hit a footballing high. My dad had told me about his mate Mark who played football, and I presumed he meant down the park on a Sunday because my dad was a bit of a bullshitter and had told me that it was him who was the bloke surfing at the start of Hawaii 5-0, lead the assault on Port Stanley to reclaim The Falklands, and was also 30th in line to the throne. As you can imagine I didn't take much notice of him. Anyway, Mark was actually Mark Dennis who played for QPR and he was probably one of the dirtiest players around at the time; he had a bad reputation both on and off the pitch.

He was actually a very good left back and if he was around in today's modern game, he would command a big fee. People will tell you he was rubbish but all they remember are the red cards, tabloid front page headlines and the blonde perm. Mark drank with my dad and his mates in a pub called 'The Rock' on the Walworth Road, but it wasn't actually a pub, it was a lunatic asylum. It seemed to attract every Millwall loon from the local area, so as you can imagine, it was a busy place.

Just as Millwall's first season in the top flight had started, my dad said we would meet Mark after the QPR game at home and he would introduce us to the QPR players. I mean they had Trevor Francis, Paul Parker and even David Seaman, all good players. But better than that he knew the Millwall player George Lawrence from his Southampton days. I don't actually know how the communication problem occurred between my dad and Mark as 'knew him' obviously didn't mean the same to my dad and Mark as it did to me. The warning signs were there before the game as he said to my dad "Watch what I am going to do to George Lawrence. I have never liked him". When he stuck poor George into the air 5 minutes into the game, I still didn't twig that my day wasn't going to be meeting my heroes. After the game (which was a cracker and saw Millwall briefly go top of the league for the first time in our history), we stood outside the away dressing room. Within 5 minutes of full time Mark came out in a blazer, and what looked like tracksuit bottoms, and said to my dad "You ready Den?". My Dad told him I wanted to wait a few minutes to get some autographs and as the QPR players came out, you could sense that he wasn't a favourite. I think I got the autographs of Simon Barker and that old carthorse who would later play for us, Mark Falco. We were then off. We did the 10-minute walk to the Canterbury Arms in record time as Mark shook hands with a few Millwall mates, but got dog's abuse from the ones he didn't know. We were even at the pub before the credits to the full-time results came up. I sat there in dismay as he knocked back pint after pint, laughing and joking. I was thinking please God, don't tell me Cas and Brian Horne do this when we lose.

I saw a few other players from opposition teams not seem to give a monkey's about the result. I clocked all this as I would always stand outside the away dressing room. I was lucky enough to meet some top dollar players and kept my boyhood footballing dreams alive. John Barnes was a nice bloke, Tony Adams a true gent, but by a country mile it was Gazza. He was bonkers, and it was the first time I had seen a mobile telephone. He was telephoning his mates and putting us on the dog (dog and bone = phone) to speak to them. He also gave kids money and talked for ages. It's so sad to see how he has gone downhill these days. The greatest English footballer of my generation, easily.

As the following years went by, I continued to be Millwall mad. I had a sense of knowing that it was only a matter of time before I started heading away with my own circle of friends like Jan, Tippler and Hotdog, and I couldn't wait. Get me on the road with the Lions.

NINE TO FIVE

After spending the summer of 1995 in beer gardens, parks and betting shops, I needed a few weeks work before I went to university. It didn't have to be anything that would set me up for life, just a few weeks work to pay off the debts I had built up over those amazing summer months. I was actually hoping for a few weeks work in the school office with my mum, but mum knew that was too easy for me, and sent me down to Camberwell Green and the Jobcentre. I was looking at the job boards and nothing was suitable. After an hour of no luck a lady called Laura introduced herself and said she was the Disability Employment Adviser. We talked about what I was hoping to find in terms of employment. I found her to be someone who was easy to talk to and she understood my aim was to work a few weeks in an office and then off, but most of all she didn't see my disability as a barrier to finding work. The confidence she gave me was a unique feeling, and I doubt I would ever have found employment so quickly and smoothly if I hadn't met Laura by chance.

After our initial meeting Laura sent me off with application forms for the Home Office, Southwark Council and bizarrely the Co-Op Funeral Directors, who were all looking for a casual administrative officer. She asked me to complete all the forms and return to the office in two days. So, 48 hours later, eager beaver Evans is sitting in the waiting area at 9.03am armed with completed application forms and a CV. My meeting lasted a few minutes and Laura promised to send all the completed forms off and would read through my CV. I felt a little deflated as I made the journey home. I was convinced I was just entering a world of knock backs or jobs where the distance was too far to travel or access to buildings was poor. My initial confidence had long gone for some reason.

A few days later Laura telephoned me. It was a quick chat to see if I had a suit and could I attend the Jobcentre for 1pm on Monday as they had 2 casual Admin Officer vacancies within the centre and the manager had read my CV and was impressed. I was buzzing; an opportunity was all I wanted and my confidence returned. I'm having this, I thought.

I attended the interview on the Monday and I played a blinder. Many people over the years have said I have the gift of the gab so I knew I had to rein it in a bit, and show them I could do the job as well as the next person and for that I needed confidence in myself. A few hours later I received a telephone call offering me the job. That was followed by a telephone call from Laura who had helped me so much, screaming with excitement. I went on to become her colleague and I'll always be grateful to her and her manager Marie for giving me a chance to show that I was as good if not better than anyone else. When my mum came home from work and I told her my good news, she cried her eyes out. This was another milestone in a Duchenne's world that she thought she would never experience as a mum. We went large that night. Takeaways, wine and laughs with my mum, step dad and brother.

***

I started on Wednesday 02.08.95. I earned that job on merit and no one gave me a pass for being disabled. The Disability Adviser helped me practically, as basically, because I couldn't see the top of the job vacancy boards, that was the only extra help I needed to be a regular member of staff like my colleagues. I felt on top of the world and will never forget the feeling of satisfaction and pride. I went for 6 weeks and stayed 16 years. Cash on the hip turns a young lad's head.

Working in the Jobcentre wasn't that bad and I never loved work, but I didn't hate it either. I was the baby of the office being in my early twenties when I first started work. My colleagues were very protective of me but never too overpowering, and I was expected to put in a shift like everyone else. There were some great characters coming through the door. Being in Camberwell and having Maudsley Psychiatric Hospital only 2 minutes away, meant we would come across some total loons, and the local area was a melting pot of weird and wacky behaviour. Violence was common and the police were called a few times a week. What I noticed from the beginning was that if someone started with threats of violence then it didn't normally materialise, but ended with verbals and an opportunity to play to the gallery. It was the quiet ones who were deathly silent that would erupt.

Yet I can count on one hand the times I was really scared. I know my mum and Kellie constantly worried about me working there and the dangers it entailed. I can remember a guy coming in and being told his payments had been stopped. He seemed to take it in his stride but as he walked away, he mumbled "I'll be back". No one was expecting Arnie, but a few hours later he walked up to the desk and unzipped a large holdall. He then pulled out a can of petrol and started pouring it over himself. If that wasn't scary enough, the box of matches he was now trying to spark sure was. Just then a have-a-go-hero colleague leapt into action and vaulted over the desk. I reversed as far away as possible at this point. Luckily my colleague managed to grab the matches and chuck them, and then, with the help of the security guards, they held him down until the police got there.

What became of the nut-job who tried to become a fireball, I don't know and I could never work out who was crazier that day. The bloke who tried to ignite himself or my colleague who saved him. This episode never made the news, they never did. Really it should have been front page but it was just another day.

Some of the best fights I witnessed were punter versus punter. Anything could set them off. Someone pushing in, a bloke eyeing up someone else's girlfriend or just being in the wrong place at the wrong time. When I started we had one Security Guard and by the time I left we had four.

I never really got that much abuse from the punters, and I'm not really sure why I got off so lightly. Maybe it was because I was in the wheelchair, but being local definitely helped; or maybe I was just a nice bloke. I would like to think it was the latter. A few times I would get the odd "fuck off", or other intelligent comments, but these were every few months. Some poor sods were getting abuse, threats and chairs chucked at them on a daily basis. I think the only run in that got to me was once when a bloke got really nasty about me being disabled. We had a reception desk. You would put your name on a list and wait to be called out. A bloke had put has name down on the list. I was due to cover the receptionist at lunch time and as I took over, the receptionist put a line through the last name. Unfortunately, he had crossed out this bloke who had been sitting for around twenty minutes. I am ploughing through the list when suddenly this bloke comes over and I just knew he was going to be a prat. A small little ginger thing with a dirty looking beard and greasy hair; he would have made a cracking extra in The Lord of the Rings.

Straight away he starts kicking off, saying I had ignored him. When I looked at the sheet and asked him his name, I thought shit, he has been crossed out. Now, I fully understand why this bloke is pissed off and any excuse I gave him was not going to make him feel any better; he was angry and wanted payback. I explained how the mistake was made, apologized and tried to deal with his query. All this bloke kept doing was issuing every swear world in the world. Then he started getting personal saying, "You only got the job because you're a spaz". That was it. It was the one and only time I really lost my rag at work. The thing is, the bloke kept going on and on. Spaz this, Spaz that. I remember some big Rastafarian in the waiting area coming over and telling him to watch his mouth. The bloke was livid and I was arguing back; in fact, I was giving it right back. The managers were on their way out. The bloke goes to me "Remember I know what time you finish work". I snapped back "Just remember I know where you live".

It was a stupid thing to say as he could have chinned me and I am a sitting duck really. My bosses didn't say too much, they just diverted me to a back office. Sometimes you'll get pushed too far in life and you'll just snap. My brother always called them my Falling Down moments after the film starring Michael Douglas.

I witnessed human nature at its worst. Some of the scumbags that darkened our doors were pure evil, but I also met some decent, genuine and lovely people. The majority fell into the second category of good people. I made some good friends. I would see people in there and then bump into them at football, in the bookies or in the pub, but you were not allowed to be friendly with the clients. The department was very old fashioned and had a 'them and us' mentality. I never really looked at it in this way. For me I was just a bloke off the Estate who was trying to get on with his life. I was raised knowing the world didn't revolve around me, so if I could help someone whilst doing my job, then of course that's what I'd do.

I met some gorgeous women from Camberwell to Colombia and Walworth to Warsaw. I made lots of lady friends through work too…

We had some good times out as well. The Friday trip to the pub is always a good sign of the morale of any office. Am I sounding like David Brent? You could argue and moan all week but if most of your colleagues could still all sit and have a pint and a laugh come 5pm on Friday, then most things could be forgotten.

Camberwell had some decent pubs and a late-night trip to the Venue in New Cross would entice the more outgoing members of the team. I remember taking one of my quieter colleagues to a place called Scribbles on the Old Kent Road. It was like the Wild West. You would regularly see stabbings, police raids etc. Everyone believes their local pub is the toughest and the area they grew up in is the roughest. I get the bravado and why people indulge in this to some extent; we've all done it at some point, but honestly, Scribbles was the Daddy of rough drinking venues.

Why did I go there? The same reason as most lads aged 17-40 did... drugs, easy women and a late drink. Looking back now, it was a stupid place to frequent, but at a young age you seem attracted to doing silly stuff. I still wonder about the bloke from work who tagged along with me and my pals from Walworth Road to Scribbles. He lasted a little under thirty minutes in there before making his excuses and disappearing into the night, and a few months later he went off on long term stress. I'm hoping still to this day that the counselling he received was work related and not linked to his visit to Scribbles.

I never really found my disability to be an issue while working. During my working day I used a tried and tested approach that I had been using since a young lad. Find a niche area and put yourself somewhere where you have specialist knowledge or can do something others can't. I've been doing this all my life; it's literally a survival tactic.

Within a few months of working at the Jobcentre (never just a dole office) I had made myself an expert on forms and how to check them, and more importantly, which ones are needed in each individual scenario. I know my JSA forms completely, the ES forms, even the Tax and Income Support forms. Then a role came up as a Training for Work payments officer. No one wanted this job as it involved you being trained in the payments and you being the person getting all the moans. No one stepped forward to apply, except the bloke in the wheelchair. I had to learn how to do this for my own self-esteem and respect. Why? Because I needed to show that even with the barriers in front of me I could still do something that others couldn't.

I studied all the books and training manuals; I even took some home to read one Sunday and I went on every training course they offered. You are 100% right, I'm a bit of a nerd and don't worry, my mates made sure they told me. But you need to see it from my side of the fence. I can't make myself useful running down to the shop or carrying boxes when a delivery has come, so disabled people need to make themselves needed and in demand. This was just my way of making myself irreplaceable.

I have to say my colleagues were excellent and they always helped me. It could be photocopying something or getting a file out of the records section; I never felt like I was a pain, but I did return the favour by doing the shit jobs they didn't want to do. If I look back at what I could do when I started, to what I could do at the end, it was heart breaking. My health had declined a lot.

So many kind people supported me. I met a good friend called Sabrina who really looked out for me when my brother died. Returning to work was made that little bit easier thanks to the colleagues I had, and football talk always managed to sneak into the office. Two good friends of mine, Steve and Paul were football mad. Paul was a Geordie and a Newcastle fanatic and I would take plenty of stick for being Millwall, but loved it. I also had a strange encounter with an ex-Millwall player while working at the Jobcentre. Regularly I would have to telephone local offices to chase up paperwork. Whenever I rang the London Bridge office, I seemed to speak with a bloke called Wesley. One day one of the supervisors called Greg said "Lee you're a Millwall supporter? Wesley at London Bridge played for Millwall". It turned out that it was an ex-Millwall player called Wesley Reid (who happened to go to my old school William Penn). We talked about Wes; he presented my brother with the Bob Cox trophy when he left primary school. Remember?

The next time we all went for a drink after work, Wesley came. As you can guess, I drove the poor bloke mad for about two hours.

One of my favourite stories was around a deputy manager called Dave. He was an ex-school teacher who treated us all like his pupils and would constantly tell you off for the slightest thing. He guarded the stock room like it was his own personal stash; every request for a new pen had to be explained in detail. One day during an office meeting he went berserk about missing pens, so, for a laugh, I asked one of my mates at another office to post a few in an envelope addressed to David. Well, after giggling in the tea room when the envelope arrived, others joined in and the word spread. Within a week it had snowballed. He was getting sack loads of pens from all over the country.

Sadly, the managers did not see the funny side and said if any more arrived they would try to trace the post mark and have the department take disciplinary action against individuals involved. It never got to the stage of formal action but would involve a lot of hassle for someone just having a laugh. To this day the sight of those Royal Mail grey sacks brings a huge smile to my face. I wonder what Dave is up to these days and if he is sweet for pens?

So how did it all end then at the Jobcentre?

The truth is my condition finally won. As much as I love to fight things to the end, I was like an old boxer who just didn't have the reflexes anymore. My breathing was getting worse and fatigue was kicking in. I had also dislocated my shoulder and this was becoming a prolonged nuisance for me on a daily basis. But before I got to the end, I was stitched up a little by some managers who wanted to get rid of me. For the management team it was all about ticking boxes and elbowing people out of the door for breaching sickness levels. It's crazy to think that in today's world of equality I would now be a protected species being disabled. Back then it was a little different. It was a case of "thanks for your time, but you can now fuck off".

I had been there for fifteen years and for over fourteen years I was more than capable of doing my job. I always maintained that if ever my health got too much I would walk, or in my case, wheel away. It only became too much in the last year. During the battle between myself and the management team, I received a fair and supportive review from the Occupational Health Service. I was allowed a higher trigger point; I went over it by a few days and the crazy thing was there were times in previous years when I had not even come anywhere near my trigger point. The people above sensed a chance to strike a mounted a campaign to get me out. I wasn't alone as I had seen them take out numerous colleagues in the same ruthless style. To be honest I was already half thinking about retiring. Both Kellie and my mum didn't want me to be working in such a potentially violent environment, and we had only just got married. I also listened to Kellie and took on board that while I had given everything to continue working, the battle was coming to an end and it was time to reinvent myself for the future and its obvious forthcoming health challenges. I also had my eye on a decent pension lump sum.

A few days on the beer had already been paid for in my eyes. Well, why not, I worked hard.

The thing is I couldn't just walk away. If they hadn't treated me like they had, I would have gone straight away without a word, but once they started questioning my ability to do my job and pulling me up on really trivial things, I did the one thing I am good at; I dug my heels in and become a stubborn little git. I played them at their own games. A diary was kept of every communication I had with managers, every email was printed out and kept in a folder at home, and if anything deviated from my job role, I would show them my job description and refuse to carry the task out. Every time I moved desks, I asked for a new work station assessment to be carried out. I also received some brilliant support from my Union, the PCS, and they backed me the whole way. I'm far from a leftie union type but the professional advice and support they gave me has made me always champion the importance of unions in the workplace.

My colleagues were also really supportive. They knew it was bollocks and had also been victims of these middle management types trying to progress to senior management. This battle really heated up during the summer of 2009. At work I would never let them think they had got the better of me or had me on the ropes. Many a time I would come home so stressed I could have cried, but within the sanctuary of our house both Kellie and my mum would keep me sane, dust me down and get ready to fight again the next day.

My mum drummed into me, "No matter what they say, don't lose your rag and never walk out".

Using my disability, and more so my condition, was a really cheap and nasty trick from the people in charge. For years I had said that when the day came that I couldn't work anymore I would be the first to know, I always would have called it a day.

Just as the battle was getting out of hand, my shoulder went and dislocated again. I remember it popping out at a Millwall v Carlisle game in early September. I can't even do justice to describe the pain that I was in and I never went back to work after that weekend in September 2009. I spoke to my Union rep and she said she thought we had proved our point and maybe now was the time to get out with a good deal. I took the maximum lump sum and a smaller monthly income. We bought a car and really found our independence. We used some of my payoff to enable Kellie to take a year's career break from her job in the NHS, and that year was priceless and the memories will live forever.

With the little bit of cash, I had remaining, well, I just spunked it; wasted it on meals out with my mum and the Mrs and all the people that looked out for me, some new clothes and booze and Millwall. Well, why not, that's what money is there for isn't it? So in the blink of an eye my boring career was over, but everything happens for a reason. The job gave me opportunities that I never thought I would have, and I will always be indebted to Camberwell Jobcentre.

TRUE COLOURS

"Acceptance doesn't mean resignation; it means understanding
that something is what it is and there has got to be
a way through it"
Michael J Fox

When you quote someone you always want to quote someone that history remembers, a powerful figure and an icon that will last forever. Churchill, Genghis Khan, even Elvis would do. A great 80's actor he may well be, but I never thought in a million years that I would find guidance from Mr Fox. It sums up my weird life that I have quoted Michael J Fox.

My acceptance of my condition came at an early age. Not sure when but I never have really had an issue with it. Of course, you get down and anyone who says that you don't is in denial.

But it is what it is?

Like Michael says above, there has to be a way through it. For me there has been changing things to work, and pushing myself on, but there has to be a way through it. Yours may be different to mine, your disability or problems may differ, but you have to find that way to fight through it.

PHOTOGRAPHS

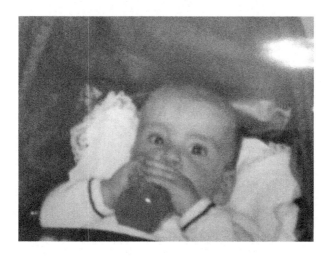

Lee aged 7 months

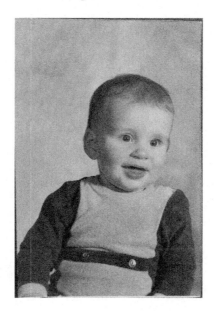

Fig 2 Lee aged 1 year

103

Lee aged 18 months with Grandad George in Setchell Road Bermondsey

Lee with his beautiful mum aged two and a half

Damiens's christening in 1978 with Father Whitelam and Mum & Dad

In Kennington with my Grandad Jock aged 3

I've been Millwall mad all my life. Me playing football in the garden aged 5

Lee and Mum on holiday in Corfu aged 7

My brother Dames aged 7

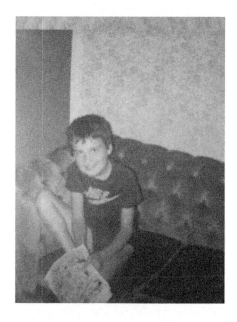

Young Lee aged 8

On holiday in Portugal with my dad aged 10

1986, what a good looking boy I was

Muscular Dystrophy sponsored walk 1985

Only 14 years old and bunking off school
to visit the Den

1989 - I was mad about England as a kid

Presentation with Millwall players after a darts marathon in the Queen Vic, Bermondsey, 1988

My 10th birthday party 1985

*Rimini 1986, Family holiday with Uncle Don
and the Kempsters*

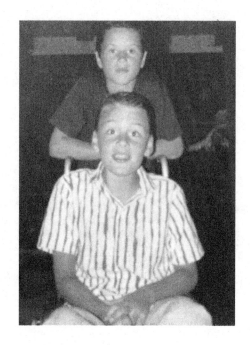

Lee and Jamie Kempster in Rimini 1986

At Lords with my main man, Uncle Billy, in 2014

*My Uncle Malc took us to meet Del, Rodney
and Uncle Albert in 1991*

On the beer with my good friend Darren Dunphy

Outside the Station Tavern, John Ruskin Street, on our way to see Millwall at Wembley, 1999

Brussels Midi Station 2006, on our way back from another Brugges trip

On the beer in Brugges 2006

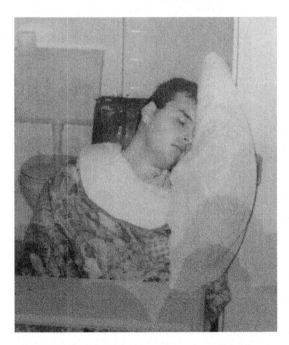

Down and out in Amsterdam 2007

Jan, Ginge, Tippler and me at Wembley,
Millwall v Wigan, 1999

Fulham away with two loveable rogues
Dean & Spanish Joe 2013

With the Duke (Dad) at Lords in 2009

My first day at William Penn - September 1986

Lads trip to Brussels for my birthday... it was a mad one! We made friends with the Belgian Police and the British Border Force in 2007

Lee, Dames and Jan with Australian Captain, Allan Border, at the Oval in 1991

THE DAY WE CAUGHT THE TRAIN

I was now reaching the age of independence and being able to go roaming with my pals. The ironic thing was that after all the years of blanking me to go with his mates to away games, my dad had now started to go full circle and wanted to tag along with us. I had left school by now and was studying for a B Tec National Diploma in Science at Putney College. I don't think this course even exists anymore, but as I wanted to be a pharmacist, I had to do two days a week work experience in Boots in Brixton for a year. What a depressing job. After dispensing methadone to junkies and haemorrhoid cream to old girls all day, I knew this wasn't the profession for me. The only good thing was the amount of time I could go missing while at Boots. Now Brixton was as rough as a bear's arse and this was long before the trendy hipster invasion, so I spent my time between the bakers and the bookies. Also, every other Tuesday afternoon I joined the legion of postmen who had finished work early to watch Millwall's reserves play at 2pm. Money was tight and my mum was a grafter, proper old school, so she made sure we didn't go without, but as a single parent with only one income, there just wasn't any spare cash. She told me and Ginge at an early age that if we wanted the extras in life then we would have to source them ourselves. I always had half a business brain and without giving myself a jolly I still do, so I decided I needed to get some weekly cash for my daily sausage roll intake at college and to pay for Millwall games, so I tried hard to sell anything

119

that came my way. As long as it wasn't drugs I was flogging, my mum didn't mind as I sold knocked off watches, meat and Jekyll (Jekyll and Hyde = snide) or nicked clothes, you name it.

But as I was reliant on the supply of local contacts it was a bit hit and miss, so I also sold lottery tickets for Millwall, and this was a gold mine. You got two free tickets for every game and I always bunked in, so I sold my two to people in the local pubs of Walworth. I also built up a handy little round to sell my tickets from the Elephant all the way down to Camberwell which was well over a mile and had lots of side streets. The trick was to do the round yourself a few times and show your face. They say God loves a trier and it seemed the people of Walworth did too, as everyone felt sorry for the young college kid out in all weathers selling his tickets. Then I discovered the concept of pyramid selling, I kid you not. I would get one of my pals to collect the winning tickets and just give them a few quid out of what I had earned. This worked for years and gave me some much-needed cash until I got a real job. I try not to look down at people, but I never seem to understand kids these days who expect other people to pay for them. There are some decent kids out there, but a lot just want a free ride and it's the reason our whole society and communities have changed.

I am far from Richard Branson, but I found a way of paying for what I wanted to do without always being on the ponce off my family.

So, with a few quid in my pocket, I could start my trips away. First up for me and my mate Jan was Watford away on a Tuesday night. We bunked college and were at Euston by 1pm. Blimey, you would have thought we were about to take a journey on the Trans-Siberian Express as so much preparation and time was put into this. We arrived in Watford at about 1.45pm, tried to get served in a few pubs and got blanked.

Luckily a few Millwall lads helped us out and got us a beer, and after a few we were pissed, so headed to the ground about two hours early. The footballing Gods smiled on us that night and we came away with a decent win through goals from Alex Rae and Paul Kerr.

By now I was hooked on Millwall away. I was honestly hooked on football in general and still am, but my love for Millwall takes it to a higher level. It's like when you have a niece or nephew and you think you love them with all your heart; well, you think you do until you have your own kid. Football is the same. That love you have for your team is at a different level and Millwall is a sick love. It can kick you in your bollocks when you are on your knees, like a bird shagging your best pal, but every now and then you will see a love in it you never knew existed. For me those Millwall orgasms were knocking Arsenal and Chelsea out of the cup, beating Sunderland in an FA Cup semi-final, and thrashing West Ham at home 4-1. You could literally watch that with Jackie Wilson singing *'Your Love Lifts Me Higher'*.

As for music and football, there is only one song. A bloke called Roy Green wrote a song called *'Let 'em Come'* and for me it just makes the hair on the back of my neck stand up. We play it at weddings, parties, christenings and funerals in our family, and as most are Millwall fans we have a good sing along. I always remember the dark days of my brother being really ill, but he would push himself on to get down The Den. As the players were warming up, he would look across and we both would be singing our hearts out. It didn't matter how shit the week had been or what we were returning to face, for those two or three minutes we were somewhere else. Only to return to the real world and another poor Millwall performance, but we expected that. So, after getting the Millwall bug and a few quid in wages in my sky (sky rocket = pocket), I had the opportunity to get to many games and I was lucky that I had a group of mates who included me in everything. It would have been easier for them to jump in a car, door to door, but they treated me the same as any other mate. As long as you bought a beer, they didn't really care about the added hard work of having to push a lump in a wheelchair around and the away games were always our favourite. It didn't matter if it was just me and my pal Jan going to Port Vale, or 20 of us going to Manchester City.

The buzz of walking into a random train station at 8am or 9am on a Saturday morning and wondering who you would bump into out of your acquaintances from an away day, was the best feeling of the week.

You make so many friendships at football that last you a lifetime. Most of my friendships have either developed through Millwall or were made there; some through a simple chat in a pub in some random town, or having a spare match ticket and getting into a conversation with the person buying your spare ticket. Carrier bags of cold Stella and a bottle of JD would have been sourced and chilled on the Friday night. If it was a dry train (where the police ban alcohol) then my bag on the back of the wheelchair would double in size, this tactic only failed once and sadly that was the FA Cup final at Cardiff when an eagle-eyed copper noticed the bag looking big. I told him it was just my piss bottle and medication but Poirot wasn't having any of it and promptly confiscated the bottle of JD, bottle of Vodka and 24 cans of Stella for the Christmas party. Some of my friendships made at football have been closer and more important to me than my family, which is hard, as I have an amazing family. An example are my friends from Bruges who have stood shoulder to shoulder at both my mum and Ginge's funeral, enjoyed my wedding and birthdays and treated my family like their own.

But it's the boys on the Manor, the lads from the pubs, train carriages and empty stadiums on our travels across this great country that matter, basically 'your own' type of people. They never judged, they just supported me and pushed me on in life. When I'm in hospital it's friends from Millwall who are there, keeping an eye on my Mrs and boy. It's what we do, as Millwall fans we might not be everyone's cup of tea, but we know how to look after our own and I've been blessed to receive that support. I often reflect on where I am in life and who has supported me to get there. I'm immensely proud of what I've achieved in my challenging life, I mean each day is a poxy battle, but I still get up and want more. Even after a shit day of pain and disappointment, I'm back the next morning wiping my mouth and asking for more.

When I sit down and take all this in, I think coming from a rough housing estate in South East London was the best thing (bar having Kellie and Jude in my life) that could have happened to me. It toughened me up and put obstacles down in front me at an early age, and that was like conditioning me for later life in a way. I honestly believe if I didn't grow up on the Pelier and Brandon Estates as a kid, but grew up on a nice suburban street,

I wouldn't be here today. I'm not for a minute saying it was like South Central LA or Compton. For me it was the whole "fuck you I'll show you" mindset. Millwall is no different at all, in fact, if the estates were my education, then Millwall is Cambridge or Oxford University as a place where you complete your education and you move on from theory to practical in the world of not giving a fuck.

Millwall means the fans and the fans' reputations make you think the worst and we are the biggest small club in in the world. Go on holiday to Greece, and Manos the waiter will ask you who you support. When you say Millwall, he won't know any players but will say "crazy fans" as Millwall has always been a broad church. You have so many odd people. At its heart you have good hardworking people who just like a beer and a laugh, aren't afraid to speak their minds and won't put up with shit, and I can't see a problem with that, but on the other hand, sometimes as fans we have gone too far and deserve our bad press, but others have done the same and got away with it. My take on all this is we sing a song called "No One Likes Us, We Don't Care". I love this attitude and will never go cap in hand to change an outsider's opinion of us. The mad thing is I have taken many friends and family friends to Millwall and they have all felt nothing but welcome.

The stand out games… There were so many good trips out following Millwall with my pals. A lot of the time the memories on our travels created better times than the drubbings on the pitch and going to Cardiff in August 1999 was a massive highlight. You always look out for how the other teams with good support are doing. For a lower league team like Millwall, a trip to Leeds, Elland Road, Bristol City's Ashton Gate, or Cardiff's Ninian Park can turn into the highlight of your season, and I had never been to Ninian Park, but had heard so many stories from older fans. It seemed like a mad house, so, when they got promoted to our division, the whole summer was spent discussing the forthcoming trip. The buzz you get on a big away day is unreal. It doesn't matter if you are an off your head loon or a bloke minding his own business, the thought of turning up en masse in a faraway town and being met with hostility gives you a unique feeling.

It was a scorching hot summer's day when we arrived. There were about 150 of us on our train and it had been kicking off in the city centre all morning, so the police told us we would be heading straight to the ground. Me and my pal pulled one of our favourite strokes, the old disabled lad needing to take his medication, so we nipped out of the police escort to find a pub. Not the greatest of ideas as we ended up in some back streets and near a pub full of meat head taffs. As we were lost, we decided to head to Ninian Park and up ahead were a few police vans, so I asked one copper for directions. He was an older bloke who should have known better and he said in a strong Welsh accent *"I can smell the fear"*. Prick, I thought, and just as my big mouth was about to get me into trouble, a policewoman jumped in to point us in the right direction. Once near the ground we caught up with the Millwall escort and it was total mayhem as Millwall was boxed in on a side street trying to get out to confront Cardiff. You had the Cardiff fans behind and in front trying to get at Millwall. There were some Cardiff fans trying to get through a park and I then witnessed something that to this day still makes me laugh. A police helicopter flew towards the approaching fans and swooped down. They all hit the deck and, honestly, it was like something from a film. Me and my pal were sitting on someone's wall when I saw a copper come marching towards me shouting. Now, being a bit mutton (Mutt and Jeff = deaf), I couldn't work out what he was aggrieved about, but I then twigged I had shorts on and had a big Millwall tattoo on my calf. He chucked us in the escort for our own safety and in fairness I walked around Cardiff for an hour amongst their fans. They would have seen my tattoo, but not said a word and that's how it should be, so in my experience they go into a unique little group with Bristol City, Chesterfield, Plymouth Argyle, and Shrewsbury Town as teams who have a few lads but don't need to start on a bloke in a wheelchair having a beer at football.

The game was as lively as the shenanigans outside. Millwall went 1-0 up through Neil Harris, Millwall's record goal scorer. As I said earlier, Cascarino was my favourite as he reminds me of some fantastic times supporting Millwall as a kid, but Harris is the man, for all he has achieved on and off the pitch, and his recovery from cancer was inspirational.

Our goalkeeper Tony Warner got into a bit of trouble for chucking a bottle back into the crowd that had been chucked at him, and the atmosphere inside was evil as you weren't really sure what was going to happen next. Only West Ham away in 2009 has ever made me feel as wary as this. We were kept in the ground for ages in the sun and their fans were outside chucking concrete over the wall at us. The walk back seemed to take a year, but it was slightly more organised, although we still had a few bottles thrown and attempted ambushes. The Millwall fans I was with seemed to have lived for that day and Cardiff in all fairness had no interest in starting on me, but my only worry in these situations is getting knocked over or crushed.

When we got back to London we got straight on the beers around Paddington and at 11pm we were looking for a sherbet (sherbet dab = cab) to get home. There was a television programme at the time called Paddington Green which was a fly on the wall documentary about the local area. One of the main characters was a Jewish wig maker called Harry and as we walked past his shop, he was standing out front. After having a chat, one of my pals, Barnard, asked him to give me a wig and he said they take time to make but said he had some customers' moustaches. Within minutes my mates had got me to agree to having a big thick Magnum P.I. style tash stuck on, but this one was ginger. It was a great laugh that night, until a few days later when I realised the glue he had used wasn't coming off and I had to walk around with this hairy slug worm above my top lip for a week.

Following Millwall was not all about the trouble that came with it. Don't get me wrong, you always seemed to encounter some hassle on away days or some wally telling you what to do, but the fact is, like most Millwall fans, we were working class lads who liked a beer and a laugh following our team, but would stand up for ourselves and each other if someone tried to take a liberty with us. I was a bloke in a wheelchair, I couldn't chuck a punch to save my life, but I just loved the whole scene. The clothes, the music, the drink and the wind ups. It shaped me into who I am today and I found that acceptance I had always wanted. The blokes who do four-hour train journeys up north liked the fact that the bloke in the chair could give as good as he got, and I wouldn't change my Saturdays up north with the chaps as a young lad for anything.

So, many times, thirty of us would be in a bleak northern town and everyone would pile out of the pub for handbags (fights) but I would be sat at the bar on my own watching the horse racing. Then, ten minutes later everyone would charge in, adrenalin pumping, all shouting, only for someone to cry out *"Who won the 2.10 at Chepstow?"*

We loved the club and we knew everything; I've always been a proper sad statto, but we all were. Millwall was ours, it was part of us and we were part of it, even if they didn't always want us.

There was no obnoxious behaviour; loud, rowdy, oh yes, but Millwall fans looked out for people. I've seen them tell others to wind it in when playing up when families got on a train going on a trip to see grandparents. Me and my little group did actually enjoy getting away from the main group of travelling fans as well. You knew the games when you wanted to get on it and have a wild one. But just as important were the relaxing away days of a small town, no hassle around you, and the reward of finding a quiet back street pub and just sitting with a few of your circle and having a good chat.

My group was always Jan, Pony, Big Paul Taylor, Hotdog, Spanish, Glassborow, Paranoid Pete and of course, my brother Ginge. It was Jan who I would sit there on a long journey with and really talk to about how hard things were, especially around Ginge being ill.

We had some cracking laughs at the away games. Away to Bristol Rovers near the end of the season in 1997, a few of us chucked in sickies at work to go to a meaningless end of season game on a Tuesday night. It was a good laugh with a few beers around Paddington in the early spring sunshine. We ended up in a pub in Bristol with a few other pals, but the game was a typical Millwall turn out and a crappy 1-0 defeat. We were pushing it to get the last London train home so had given a local taxi driver a nice tip and a promise of another one if he got us back to the train station on time. Well, our Worzel cab driver had the engine running outside the away turnstiles at full time and we raced back to Bristol Parkway. Once there we had a bit of time to kill due to the unexpected driving ability of our own Lewis Hamilton, and my mates spotted the guard's room open. One went in and picked up a hat and jacket belonging to a member of staff then started putting it on me. I picked up the plastic baton the guards use, as within seconds I was being pushed onto a platform and a few Millwall fans were trickling in through the entrance. By now I had found a whistle in my newly acquired jacket pocket and was making good use of it. I have a bit of a big cannister (head), so the hat was perched on top of my head. Members of the public were coming and asking me questions about changing at obscure places like Didcot with my mates out of sight and obviously laughing. I could see a guard on the other platform who was not impressed and by the time he made it over, the remaining Millwall fans had arrived with their police escort. The guard was furious and was asking the police to arrest me for theft, so things were escalating fast and my pals were trying to remove the uniform quicker than they had got it on. Luckily the Millwall fans around made their feelings clear that it was a bloke having a laugh; also the people waiting for the train saw the funny side and also got involved. We were ushered onto the train as soon as it arrived and my brief stint of working on the railways was over.

It was the treks to places we would never have normally visited that always created everlasting memories. An example of this was York City. We went there on a Tuesday night in August and expectations were high, having just been relegated from the 1st Division. A few of us went to Bootham Crescent on this lovely warm summer's evening and we got up to York early. We had a look around the ground for a pub and stumbled across the York Supporters Club built on the side of the pitch. We finally encountered some of that famous northern hospitality; no one wanted to start on us, far from it, and we were made to feel welcome. They even let us open the fire exits and sit on the edge of the pitch and have a beer in the sun. I have always thought that if you treat people with respect then they will respond. Of course, Millwall have a few who play up, but most will respond to being treated fairly. The game itself was typical of the rubbish dished up by our then manager Jimmy Nicholl. He promised a lot but never delivered and we went 2-0 up, only to lose 3-2 to a poor York team. The only stand out moment from the match was me getting into an argument with one of our injured players. We had signed Dave Sinclair from Scotland and I think Jimmy Nicholl just thought Millwall fans are thick, so if I sign a big lump who talks tough, they will lap it up.

Nicholl on Sinclair, *"So tough he has tattoos on his teeth"* was a favourite of mine. Truth is, he never lived up to it and was always injured, so after going 3-2 down, the Millwall fans were

130

going mental. I remember screaming at one of our players to show some passion, and Sinclair behind me lent across to tell me to pipe down. Now I am nothing special but after travelling to Yorkshire on a Tuesday night, I wasn't going to have some sweaty (sweaty sock = jock) start putting me in my place. Only one response was ever going to come out of my mouth, *"fuck off"*. Reading this you probably think it's wrong for me to respond like that, even more if you aren't a football fan, but you need to understand how much this means to people.

Sinclair was taking the piss by trying to put me in my place and there were many big able-bodied men saying a lot more than me, but he took the cheap option, or so he thought. Our exchange went on for a while; he was a gobby shit who's take on the situation was that we should be lucky to have him and his pals playing for us. At the end he drifted away from the group of fans he was sitting near, a bit like how his career just drifted away.

York was such a good jolly that the next time we played them, more of us went. My brother Ginge much preferred the days out when it was more relaxed. On this trip we sat in the same stand as before, the front row of their main stand. We had signed Stuart Nethercott on loan from Spurs the day before, and he marked his debut by blazing the ball out of touch and hitting my brother point blank in the face from six feet away. Ginge was knocked spark out cold in his wheelchair.

During all of this time we didn't taste any success following Millwall. The highs were a few good cup runs in the late 90s.

Beating Arsenal and Chelsea were nights out that will live on forever and Chelsea away was brilliant. We were still kids really. I mean my brother used his remaining Christmas money (he was double tight) to pay for a sherbet over there, and we went with my pals Jan and Tippler. It was freezing and when we got out as near as we could to Stamford Bridge you could sense something in the air. It was an evil atmosphere (only that Cardiff game and West Ham away in 2009 would eclipse this). We didn't have tickets as Chelsea had refused to sell disabled tickets to away fans on safety grounds, and I doubt they would get away with this in today's world, but to be fair to them the logic was more than understandable, but I was going anyway. Once near the entrance to the big main stand at the Bridge we left it as late as possible, and for the moment of maximum disorder nearby, to make our move. We would only have one chance at this and the balance of the leaving late and seeing as many punches being exchanged was our key to success. At about 7.20pm, with military precision, we struck. The steward let us in, but was more concerned with what was going on outside. When we told him the rest of our party had all the tickets. He told us to just go inside so we were in! So close to kick off the ground seemed not even a quarter full, at kick off it was half full, but 20 minutes in you couldn't move.

My dad was in with his pals at the away end, and we kept our heads down as we were surrounded by loads of Chelsea fans, so we watched the game feeling lucky to have got in. Early in the 2nd half, our Aussie striker, Dave Mitchell, who looked like a cross between Jeremy Beadle and Barry Gibb, chased a ball out of play and fell onto the advertising boards about 2 feet away. As he was an ex-Chelsea player, he was getting dog's abuse and for a split second I forgot myself. I jumped up and went *"Come on Mitch, get stuck in"*. To my amazement and in the noise of 25,000 fans he heard me, so as he ran away, he said, *"Come on you Lions"* and you could see the Chelsea fans around me thinking, did I just hear that correctly?

The game was a classic cup tie with the start of the new Chelsea under Hoddle. We had a good team though, with some of the best Millwall have ever had. Keller, Thatcher, Rhino Stevens and Alex Rae are Millwall legends. After going a goal down, we nicked it back to 1-1 and how the temporary stand Millwall were in didn't collapse, I will never know. When we won the penalty shootout with possibly the best 5 penalties I have ever seen taken, it was turning into a war zone. Fans on the pitch with police on horses trying to regain control. But forget all what happened off the pitch, that night that was a cup turn over that our grandchildren will be talking about and luckily, I was there with my brother and my pals to see it.

When Millwall played Manchester City at Maine Road in February 1999, any football fan who had travelled with their team expected fireworks at this match and Maine Road was a ground I had wanted to visit for years. The match at The Den had been well anticipated as Manchester City were a giant of a team and had crashed out to the 3rd tier but would now be playing the likes of Millwall, Chesterfield and Bristol Rovers.

The City fans were turning up at smaller grounds like Macclesfield, Northampton and Notts County in huge numbers; in most cases it was like a home game for them. Like Leeds United, another big club who have seen poor times, they had a reputation for being bullies and taking over towns just because of the sheer number of fans that followed them. I was really looking forward to this game as even after relegation they still had a good side. Nicky Weaver was in goal with Kevin Horlock and Lee Bradbury, I seem to remember. We didn't have the greatest team then, and it was Keith Stevens' first season as manager. We had some good youngsters coming through, but what we had was the heart of a lion running through that team and I always loved getting down The Den early for these games. It was a nice early autumn evening and you can always tell when it's a big game for Millwall as you bump into some obscure Millwall fans that haven't been back since the last lively game. All the rumours were of Manchester City taking Bermondsey over, and as a regular I knew there was more chance of me scoring the winning goal. Our average crowd that season was 6,000 and the official crowd was over 12,000 with just under 2,000 away fans, but the actual figure of Millwall fans was higher.

The match was one of those games at The Den where I literally thought I could walk, and I'm serious. The buzz of the crowd, the intensity and pure raw passion. It was one of those nights where you wouldn't be surprised by anything that happened both on and off the pitch and if you told me Marilyn Monroe was serving the pies with Elvis doing the half time entertainment, I wouldn't have been shocked. The Den is unique on these occasions. Myself and Ginge were tucked in with about 12 of our lot going mad, screaming at every challenge. Early in the second half, Neil Harris scored and the place erupted. After we had a player sent off, we were hanging on for the win, only for them to grab a late equaliser. After the game, most seemed to be happy to stand around and say goodbye to the travelling fans and we went home talking of one thing, the return match.

The next few months would see the early days of internet PR and propaganda from our friends in the north who were obviously unaware of the dangers of pulling the lion's tail, and the trip to Maine Road couldn't come soon enough. But two weeks before, disaster struck when Millwall had been declined disabled tickets on safety grounds, but there was no way myself or Ginge was missing this game and we would have gone without tickets. Ginge was seeing a girl from Oldham at the time and he had the tickets sent to her address. When the tickets arrived, you had the classic "Do you want the good news or bad news?" question. The good news is we sourced two wheelchair and four normal seating tickets. The bad news was it was in the Umbro stand at the far end of the ground, furthest away from the Millwall fans...

The night before the game I remember going to Liam Ogs, our local pub, with my mates Jan and Tippler. The pub was were packed and everyone was talking about going to Manchester the next day. The next morning we arrived at Euston early, and overheard the police say a train had just left with over 300 Millwall fans on it. We looked around to see every man and his mad dog was still here, and you just knew this was going to be one of those days. We boarded the train and noticed a worrying sign; my dad was drinking already, and if he was on the beer before Watford Junction we were in for a long day. We had a warning system called the pint-ometer and how much beer he was spilling would show how pissed he was. On the train at

Milton Keynes his can of Stella was tipping everywhere. By the time we got to Stockport, the majority of the train was on its way to a level of anticipation only Millwall, birds and hard drugs can induce, and on the platform at Stockport, as we pulled in, there were around two hundred lads all looking the part. Everyone jumped up. *"Who is it? City waiting for Millwall or Cockney Reds even?"* But as the speed of the train slowed, we all started to recognise Millwall fans. They had travelled up earlier and by all accounts had annihilated the Mancunians who were awaiting their arrival. As we got off the train, handshakes and shouting out to reacquainted friends was all you could see and hear. This train was the real deal and this was what Millwall was about. At Manchester Piccadilly we came out of the escort to find an off licence and some taxis. Not all of the boys got out, but myself, Ginge and three of the boys did, also my dad. We got to the ground about fifteen minutes before the Millwall fans passed and it was the longest fifteen minutes of my life, as my dad talked in a loud South East London accent while having more beers. My dad is a constant piss taker and joker and is actually quite funny, but once he has had a beer though he can go on and on constantly non-stop. Some can handle it, just as many can't. We were standing around to meet the escort as we had been split up from the rest of our group and were standing quite near the Blue Moon Chippy. We then moved to what looked like a smallish club shop. As I turned around, I could see a really fat Manchester City fan who must have been at least 24 stone and I knew I had to keep my dad talking with the hope he didn't clock the bloke but within a few minutes he turned around and saw him. *"Blimey big 'un, you've had a few hot pots haven't ya?"* You have to factor into this story that there's only six of us here and two of us are in wheelchairs, therefore my diplomatic skills would be put to the test this day. The big fella let it go but he had a couple of pals with him. Next thing he starts looking at scarves and various bits for sale on a stall when a deep South London voice bellows out, *"Big un, Eddie Large has returned a Kappa tracksuit and it's too big for him. You might squeeze into it".* As he marched over with his mates, the Millwall escort turned into the street and an army of Robo Cops thwarted the advance of the big fella, but to be honest I was never too worried about my dad as he could more than handle himself.

We were now in between the Millwall fans and Manchester City fans. It was an army that Millwall had assembled that day and was untouchable. The sheer noise, intimidation and aggression were at levels I hadn't experienced before, and it was all being played out in the surroundings of one of Britain's roughest areas. As the Millwall fans walked past, people were calling out *"Gentle!"* to my dad as the older lot were out in force. Any chance of us passing as neutral fans on a 'footy trip' had been blown out of the water. My dad drifted off with friends into the away end, so me and Ginge headed towards the stand we had tickets for. With us that day was a mate called Raven and he is actually my wife's cousin. He isn't even a Millwall fan, but often came because his mates were going and he liked a beer and a laugh. He is like Peckham's version of Liam Gallagher, all arms and swagger as he walks; he can't fight. He thinks he can, but he can't, but credit where credit is due, he will always have a go.

The gates to the stand are open, it's about five minutes into the game and we walk in. Today was always going to be backs against the wall both on and off the pitch and the team dug in until half time to keep it at 0-0. Us, we lasted three minutes at best while Raven's arms are swinging about like a windmill as we walked along the front of the stand towards the corner flag. In fairness we could have easily been remembered from outside the ground as a few City fans were standing up telling us to fuck off. Some were coming towards us and the stewards and police came from everywhere. After some discussion they said they would take us to the away end so I presumed we would leave the ground and walk around via the street. This was not the case and we were told to follow the copper in charge. Now Maine Road is a great old football ground. So much history with some impressive stands; the Kippax is one of the iconic football stands, it's up there with the Kop, the Clock End and Cold Blow Lane. As we walked towards it and got closer, it just got bigger and bigger. As we started to walk down in front of the Kippax Stand, it was clear we were Millwall fans and it started off with verbal abuse, then all the wanker signs. I was thinking this is a bit much ain't it? As we approached the final fifty metres, the objects started raining down, like coins and lighters, and as we got to the last 20 metres, we ran into a storm by the corner flag and the Millwall and City fans were exchanging everything and anything that could cause harm. The week before the match I had received a tax rebate and there would only be one port of call to spend this on, a trip up the West End to Woodhouse where I treated myself to a new Stone Island jacket. It cost me a King's Ransom and from nowhere a cup of hot chocolate came flying towards me. Luckily it wasn't boiling hot, but it was still hot enough for me to start jumping around and indulging in some rather strange body movements. I managed to get most of the drink off without too much damage, but sadly the jacket never seemed to recover from the direct hit it had received. We had made it to what we thought was the sanctuary of the away stand, and were moved from the first few rows of seating so riot police could stand there. We moved to a little gangway between the stands, but we still had coins raining down. A copper told us to leave the stadium as we were back and forth so many times. You lose your sense of time in these adrenalin-fuelled matches and I felt like we had been in the ground for hours, but when I looked up it was only 20 minutes into the game. We found a little walkway which was literally on the corner of the Kippax Stand but by an emergency door. This secluded safety area kept us away from the projectiles, but my view was obscured by the size of the structure we were perched on the corner of. I had one eye on the game and another on the City fans to the left of us. Luckily, they were focused on the Millwall fans who were on the other side of them.

As a rule, I always have clear recollections of games I've attended, not even being pissed means I'll fail to remember the major moments, but for this match there isn't much of a match report. To be fair I was trying to stay out of harm's way and only had a view of about 40% of the pitch, but what I do remember is us hanging on until half time. We were quite an attacking team and I remember the more cultured Lucas Neil playing over the direct attacking Paul Ifill, both players that I liked. I could see the logic of playing Lucas as he was better at retaining possession which would have been so important in a game where we would be under the cosh from the start, but the plan never worked. Early in the second half we seemed to tire and our veteran keeper Nigel Spink had a poor game. Once the first goal went in the writing was on the wall, and the rest of the visit would see us flicking between Millwall hanging on to prevent a whipping on the pitch, and us watching the shenanigans between the two sets of fans. At the final whistle I was shocked at how quick we were all let out as the Millwall fans' coaches had been smashed badly. We had given one of our cab drivers a good tip to return and pick us up but as only one wheelchair could get in the taxi it would mean one of us hanging around with a few of the boys while the others went back to the train station. I took on big brother duties and said I would let Ginge go first, I'm good like that!

We were told to head to Wilmslow Road in Rusholme. You can't miss it, he said, as its Manchester's Curry Mile and I was thinking there could be worse places to be stranded for an hour. While walking through the back streets of Manchester, all I could think was that this taxi ain't going to turn up. Our position of just behind the Millwall escort, close enough to feel safe, but away so we could slip off to meet the taxi was precarious. Missiles are going in both directions and as we turn the corner, my telephone rings, it was a struggle to hear him through all of the noise, but it was the taxi driver. He had also enlisted another taxi so we could get both chairs in, so escorted by the boys we were in the taxi and on our way within ten minutes.

The trip home on a rare football special was fantastic. On our return the media slaughtered Millwall fans, but I never get too worked up about that. As I've said earlier, we sing "No One Likes Us We Don't Care" and I certainly don't. My brother decided to write to Manchester City to complain, his point being that if they had allocated us disabled tickets in advance, we wouldn't have had all the hassle we did, but if I'm honest I'm sure it was always going to be a tricky day. There was so much bad blood between the two teams and also the wheelchair enclosure was poorly designed. His letter was passed to head of security and these positions are normally held by ex-high-ranking police who want to boost their pension while still enjoying a power trip. This fella was no different, he replied to my brother and went straight on the attack with "My security staff remembered your entourage entering the stadium. Not at any point did your friends try to disguise the fact you were Millwall fans, quite the opposite. A senior steward with over 25 years of disabled matchday experience stated the two of you were the most difficult disabled fans he has encountered". He then went on to say he was sending the letter to Millwall (grass), the Sports Minister, and a list of other people. The thing is, neither myself or Ginge fell into society's image of a disabled football fan. We dined out on the letter for a while and took it to the pub before the next home game for someone to read out. I know, I know, but when you are young you love things like that and that day was what football is all about. If you only ever watch it on Sky, then you're probably scratching your head thinking ok, you've travelled halfway across England in the cold to see a match, had objects chucked at you and endured your team losing 3-0 to a team you dislike. While you may have a point, there are always two sides to a story. For me and also my brother we were living a life, we were part of something and the energy and confidence it gave us both was priceless. I still think of that trip today and I still hear people talk about that game over twenty five years later.

The wheelchair never held me back. I'd love some of my old determination in these middle-aged days; it's still there when needed, just a bit harder to fire up.

When Mark McGhee become Millwall manager I was not that impressed. He was always a little dour and had a reputation for jumping ship. By the time he departed I had witnessed some of my most enjoyable football following us as we had a cracking team with good attacking wide men in Paul Ifill and Christophe Kinet. Tough lower league players who had reached a peak with us in Nethercott, Sean Dyche and Robbie Ryan, goals through the legend that is Harris and class acts that would go onto the top flight in Timmy Cahill, Lucas Neil and Steven Reid. We had also signed Steve Claridge who was my brother's favourite footballer. The Den around that time was immense and I literally remember some teams giving up as soon as they arrived. Promotion was always looking promising under McGhee and he took us straight up as we clinched promotion at Wrexham. I can't really tell you much about that game, as, to my brother's annoyance, I drank a bottle of JD on the way up, but the important passages of the game that day are cherished. So many Millwall fans had got in without tickets, they climbed over into the empty side stand we were in and when they started running towards the Wrexham fans on the other side of me, I was so smashed I just sat there. I was the meat in the sandwich of a few hundred football fans playing up and it didn't really hurt until I sobered up.

Every football fan also has a fetish. Some collect programmes, others love non-league grounds, yet mine was always European football. As a kid I was Millwall mad but also in love with watching the European teams on Sportsnight. When my parents got us Sky, we found an early satellite channel called Screen Sport which opened up the Spanish League and once Channel 4 started showing the Italian football, I was off on a roll. I loved the whole different world to it all with the stadiums and the fans. I have no regrets about my life, but the one thing I look at is travel. I loved geography and my love of football would have linked to this, but even though getting around was difficult, I have still visited some good stadiums. A trip to Lille with my brother to see Racing Lille v Olympique Lyon was a cracking trip. By chance, Ike Turner was staying in our hotel after a concert, and somehow we managed to get into his entourage and meet him. He said to myself and my brother "I feel your pain brother" and on our return we told our mum who was disgusted that we even spoke with him after he had treated Tina so badly. I have been to Club Bruges many times where I have made many lovely friends. I went to the European Championships in 2000 and ended up drunk in Eindhoven and in the Swedish end for their game against Turkey. I made an attempt to see England play in Cologne in the 2006 World Cup too. Once in Cologne the beer gardens alongside the mighty river Rhine on a sunny day proved too much temptation for us and we decamped there. I also took my beautiful wife to Paris for our 40th birthdays and I still managed to sneak in a visit to Paris Saint Germain's Parc de Princes Stadium which has always been on my bucket list. So, when in the summer of 2000, Millwall Manager Mark McGhee used his connections in Germany (he had played for Hamburg in the mid-80s) to arrange a friendly with Eintracht Frankfurt, I was there. The minute it was announced that was it, I was there. Five of us booked to go but I couldn't fly so I worked out a route using Eurostar to Brussels, then an Intercity train to Cologne and a change there onto Frankfurt. It was a long journey and to do it in a day was probably highly unrealistic, but we were desperate to get out there. The Eurostar leg was easy, comfy seats in 1st class as the loon who had designed their trains had forgotten to put a wheelchair space in standard class and we had the pleasure of going VIP with free food and booze. Once in Brussels we re-enacted a scene from what seemed like every one of our trips anywhere and we missed the train because we were in a pub. I love a beer, but it drove me mad as it was always me who had to be wheeled out to do the talking to some train guard and explain why a group of us were travelling on tickets that were no longer valid.

The second leg to Cologne started to get heavy as we had been drinking for hours. We were stuck in the guard's van as there were no spaces for wheelchairs. This journey was spent sharing some strong skunk with an old German hippy on a bike we had befriended. During the journey I got a telephone call from my brother. Mobile telephones were not the must have item that they are today, and I wasn't going to take mine. My brother had telephoned to say the match was cancelled due to German police having security fears and at first, we thought he was on a wind up, but to be fair I was sure he wouldn't joke about something like this. Once off the telephone we contacted a pal in London to see what he would say, and straight away he informed us that the game was cancelled. We were gutted. We had gone all that way for nothing.

We finally made it to Frankfurt around 10pm, tired after our day travelling, so we just wanted to hit the hotel and get some sleep, but we had a rather large welcoming committee on the platform in Frankfurt in the shape of about 30 policemen. Their sole interest was to get us to return to wherever we had travelled from and we tried explaining that our return Eurostar from Brussels was not for 2 days so we would be better off staying in Frankfurt where we at least had a hotel. This didn't seem to be cutting the mustard with them and we were repeatedly told *"Go home to England, no fun for you here,"* even a few local Krauts on the train tried standing up for us. After about 30 minutes of arguing and the police checking we had hotels, they finally let us through under the instructions to head straight to the hotel. The next morning what were we to do? We were in a foreign city with cash on the hip. We started walking around and went to an Irish bar opposite the station. It never ceases to amaze me that your English football fan will head straight to an Irish bar once outside of Blighty. It's like heading for an Embassy when in trouble abroad. On approaching the bar, we noticed that we were not the only Millwall fans around. There must have been a good two hundred or so and many well-known Millwall boys. From early morning it seemed the plan was to just stay put, drink and enjoy the sun, but for me and my pal we knew at some point we would want to have a nose about and when we were told Frankfurt's Red Light District was a few streets away, we were like a rat up a drainpipe. Off we went to be greeted by the biggest porn shop I have ever seen. I have made many trips to Amsterdam, Brussels and Antwerp but this was on a different level. I always thought the Germans were pervs but this was something else. It must have been bigger than HMV on Oxford Street, and you didn't seem to have brasses in windows like the other cities. We went into this hotel and were given a folder. I suppose today it has been replaced with an iPad, and in the folder was a catalogue of photographs of some tidy birds. The system was to pick a bird, then on her page it would have the room number, you then went to reception and said room 146, for example. You paid for your room and then went up and did your business. It seemed a classy establishment to be fair, but we knew there were other places, so went for a walk. As we walked past what looked like a restaurant, these two girls tried to get us in inside and after a few minutes of discussions, in we went. Once inside they split us up. My last words to my pal were "Don't buy them any drinks" as I knew this was how they stitched you up. I made use of the facilities and the hospitality of my host. When she asked if I was going to buy her a drink, I said no, and she came back a few minutes later with a drink saying, "Your friend is more generous than you, he has bought me and my friend a brandy". As soon as I heard this, I knew we were fucked, twice. As soon as I got out, I called him from outside the little sectioned off bit he was plotted up in and he confirmed he had bought four brandies and two beers. When the bill was placed, we were looking at £400, gone just like that, and don't forget we had already sorted the birds out with dough. Trying to take control of the situation, I told them we only had £100 on us. Straight in they replied we take cash cards, but there was no way these cheeky fuckers were going to get my Barclaycard. Jeez, could you imagine what they would have done to it? We started making our way out and were told if we didn't pay, they would call their security, but it was a chance we were willing to take at that point. I thought even though it's hard to push a chair and run I doubt these birds will chase us if we started to run. As we started to make a move towards the door, they called

146

Gunther. This bloke, who must have been nineteen stone of all muscle, appeared in front of us. What we noticed first was the tight fitting cut down jeans he had on; he looked like the Incredible Hulk on steroids. It still hurts me today that he relieved us of our dough and we did put up some token gestures of dispute, but it got us nowhere. The only thing I can say is when we told the Millwall fans of our experience I believe the place got a visit on their walk about town on the night and Gunther couldn't get the shutters down quick enough.

We were polo and hungry. I did have my Barclaycard on me so I made a cash withdrawal to take out for beers and found the poshest restaurant we could find. An Indian called Gaylord, which made us laugh, but it had branches in Mayfair, Paris and San Francesco and was absolutely lovely. On returning to the bar, we heard that it had come under constant attack from Skinheads and Millwall being Millwall, the fans warmed to the invitation. I had returned just in time to see ex-England player Tony Woodcock attempt to carry out a PR exercise on behalf of Eintracht Frankfurt. Woodcock had played in Germany for Cologne and had started working for Frankfurt. The appearance of trying to build bridges with the pissed off Millwall fans who had travelled halfway across Europe for a game to be cancelled didn't go well. The two bob token pennants and key rings didn't seem to be appreciated, but I was literally on my hands and knees trying to get as much free merchandise as I could. On the night we headed for a walk towards the train station, a scuffle broke out between a few of my pals and some big Skinheads. The Skinheads came back in more numbers and were taking a bit of a liberty. One of our group was taking a pasting from a few of them and used a CS gas cannister to even things out. Normally most Millwall I knew didn't carry any weapons but after what we had seen that day, a few had armed themselves and that decision was now looking like a wise one.

We all seemed to get split up as the fight was being dragged all over the place and when the police arrived both camps tried having it on their Bromley's (Bromley By Bows = toes). We would later find out that not everyone was that successful. Me and my pal got back to our hotel room and were in shock from the savage attack we had witnessed. Remember we were both from a rough part of London and had seen many brutal fights growing up, but this was still shocking. The Skinheads knew exactly what they were doing and had taken a major liberty against five blokes on their own.

We sat up talking for a bit and were awaiting the return of the other three. After an hour and no sign of them, we went for a walk around. The streets were deserted but you could still feel the tension in the air and hear the police sirens in the distance, but still no sign of the boys. We finally got back without them in the early hours and as we were leaving early that morning, we tried to get some sleep. I had to sleep in my wheelchair as the hotels never had an electric bed or overhead hoist. I was fast asleep when I felt someone push me in the arm and shout *"Wake up"* in a strong German accent which sounded false. Convinced it was the boys I told them to *"fuck off"*. The next thing I felt this almighty blow across my arm. It ran from my neck to my foot at the speed of light. My eyes bulged open to see around seven policemen and a policewoman in our room. They were shouting at me to get up, dragged the duvet off me and you could see the horror and confusion when they realised I was disabled and in a wheelchair. In fairness they were apologetic and the concern of one of the policewomen who was an absolute sort, was very comforting. They were searching our room and that in itself was a worry. They wanted the passports of two of our travelling party but we played dumb and said we didn't know where they were. Unfortunately, they were next to the coffee table in a neat pile about 10cm from the copper asking the questions. Once they found the passports they were after, they were gone, and about an hour later my pal Spanish returned saying two of the lads had been nicked but only one of them would be charged.

That morning we started the return leg of a very long journey back to Blighty with all of us thinking about our pal who was looking at an extended holiday in Germany for a good few months.

Getting to games was always a nightmare until an amazing woman become first my girlfriend, then my wife, and forever my best friend. She got us a car with disabled access and when I finally had the cash to buy a car I didn't know where to start.

I have certain subjects in life that remind me of those political marches where people are just shouting so much you end up turning off to the opinions as it becomes deafening. Cars, boxing and self-pity are three examples for me where people just go on and on to share what they know. I know these seem bizarre, but I have always believed it. I'm sure you have your own subjects.

We started looking online as Kellie actually knows a bit, so this was a start, but I have no interest at all in cars and even less knowledge. My Uncle Malc knew quite a bit as he was a props buyer for television programmes working on The Bill and Only Fools and Horses, to name two. He gave us some very useful tips and was available to give us some input once we found something we liked. We were drawn to the Renault Kangoo and we test drove a few, but all that did was make us feel like we needed one urgently; yet the hard sells put us off. Then one day we noticed a silver one in a garage in Herne Bay, a town I would later move to. The owner offered to drive it up for a test drive and he arrived one Thursday evening around 7pm and an hour later he was getting a bus to Victoria to get a train home. I spent my last £5,000 pension pay off and the Silver Bullet, as we christened it, was here. Now it was time to get out and about.

She has sat in car parks waiting for me to come out of grounds on a weekly basis, but always has one stipulation to the agreement. Come out at the time agreed. What drives her mad is if I ask her to pick me up at 6.30pm from a pub and one of the boys wanders out at ten to seven saying *"Kell, he's just finishing his beer babes. Do you want a bag of crisps and a coke while you're waiting?"* To be fair it would result in me finally coming out at around 8pm to face the music. Just tell me what time and I don't care, she would say.

I have probably forgotten how hard it was before the Mrs and her chauffeuring service.

For home games me and my brother relied on a community transport service run by Transport for London called Dial a Ride. These drivers were brilliant, and I used them to travel to work. The drivers were good people and locals who you could have a laugh and joke with. One of my good friends, Roger Ousby, became a driver, and you will struggle to find a nicer bloke than Roger. A pure gent with a heart of gold and once he became a driver it was brilliant as we could deviate from the agreed trip and get him to drop us all over London. Me and my pal Chandler would find the most obscure place for him to try and reverse this massive minibus into.

Getting a booking to take you to football was hard work. You would need to telephone a booking number a week in advance, but it would sometimes take two hours to get through. You had no guarantee you would get a booking so I would forever be at work avoiding clients at 9.30am so I could use the telephone, then a massive cheer would go out as I was told I had our booking for the game a week on Saturday at home to Bristol Rovers.

As it was a community-based service, you had to share it with the local pensioners, so midweek games were a total nightmare. They had targets and obviously needed to reach those trip targets, so, for a 7.45pm match we would get dropped off at 5.30pm and picked up at 11pm which was a nightmare as it didn't give me enough time to go home. Did we ever miss a game though? Of course not. It made me laugh when we would go and stand out for hours after waiting for our lift home, yet some of our friends with cars or who lived nearby would tell the world how big a fan they were but never went. On the occasions Dial a Ride couldn't take us we would walk it. It's a good two miles from my house to The Den but myself and my brother have some good pals who always got us to games and we would hang around for a black taxi, but they don't like stopping in South East London late at night. Getting around the country by public transport was a minefield, especially in the late 90s and early 2000s but facilities have improved so much.

As a group of young lads following Millwall away, we would meet at mine for away games at 8.30am as a rule. It was my house and I was always late, much to the annoyance of my pals. We would then walk to a pub on the Walworth Road called Liam Ogs for 9am to wait for taxis to come along and as we were still at the mercy of your London cabbie, you could wait ten minutes or over an hour, but every week was the same, trying to get money out of the ponces and tight fuckers in our group for beers and taxis. Once we had a kitty, someone would run over to Costcutter opposite to grab beers and a few miniature JDs for me. Food never really came into the equation, but if you were lucky, it was a burger from BK at the train station.

Train fares have always been extortionate. Like any normal working-class bloke, we didn't want to line the pockets of big businessmen as our wages were for our days out and pals. Jibbing, as it is known, is bunking the fare. Being a football fan of a club with a poor reputation and a good away following means you only have to jib 50%. Reason being if you are in some northern soulless town like Blackburn and the police have 600 Millwall fans to get back to London they don't bother checking the tickets, it's way too much hassle. So, if you can get there without a ticket, you have made the promised land, saving a bullseye in cash. Jibbing is an art form and you have so many tactics to use. The Cat and Mouse - where you are up and down hiding in toilets, getting off one train and changing carriages. For me it was too much hassle but my good friend Sam Barnard has mastered this one to a T.

You have the Frank Abagnale, which is based on lies and the character from the film Catch Me If You Can. For this you need some balls and be quick thinking. But for myself and Ginge it was the Yoda. It was very similar to the Frank Abagnale as it was built on a lie, but the difference being that we used a Jedi mind trick to disperse any thoughts of us being on the Jib. These are not the Jublees you are looking for. How we did it was to keep our story simple and as close to the truth as possible, so on a train journey to some game one day an old couple in a wheelchair got on at Euston. Me and Ginge were behind them on the platform and as we tried to get on you could see the guards were in a panic. They explained there are only two wheelchair spaces on the trains, one in standard and one in first class. They put my brother in first class and I was left to sit outside the smelly toilets for the journey. When the guard came around, I had a moan about having to pay to sit outside a toilet and he informed me I should have been advised to travel on the next train in comfort. There and then the plan was hatched. We just wouldn't buy a ticket but would just say our party had been split up and the people on the advance train held the tickets. It was so simple and that is why it succeeded. As long as you had done your research and knew the time of the train before, it couldn't fail. We always travelled as the OFFICIAL Millwall Disabled Supporters Club and when asked who was holding our tickets, we would just say a man called Jock (this was my grandad's name and he was as straight as they come. When we told him we used his name he found it hilarious). If you were on the 11.34am to Nottingham, all you had to say was three of us tried to get on the 10.34am to Nottingham, but there was only space for two wheelchairs and 80% of the time the guards would apologise and walk off. If the guard started questioning you, just don't be rude. I learned this from work that once someone is rude to you it makes it personal.

After heading off all over the country with myself and two pals getting a free trip, we even took it to a new extreme. On a trip to Plymouth on the opening day of the 2004/05 season, myself and my pal Jan were polo (Polo Mint = skint). I think we had about £40 between us. It was a lovely summer's day and we decided to go on the spur of the moment. We must have done about £25 in the cab to Paddington, and when we got on the train for what was a mammoth journey lasting over 4 hours, we knew the remaining £15 wasn't going to get many beers in and certainly no grub. As we approached Reading a female guard came around, I did my usual speech and this very nice girl lapped it up. "Sir this is disgraceful. Would you be offended if Great Western moved you to First Class as a gesture of good will?" My nan always told me never to look a gift horse in the mouth, so, of course, we accepted their very generous offer and had a lovely liquid lunch topped off with a truly amazing beef and horseradish sandwich. As we were getting nearer to Plymouth and with the beers flowing, we were trying our hardest to chat the guard up. She asked us why we were off to Plymouth but sticking to the rule of keeping it simple, we told her for football, and we were returning that night. She came back saying that Great Western had put on a taxi for us to get to Home Park and it would collect us after the game at 5.30pm and return us to the station. On top of all that the taxi drove straight into the Main Stand at Plymouth, and we sneaked in for free and got a transfer to the away end.

We witnessed a boring 0-0 draw in the sun and got the cabbie to stop at the offie on the way back to use the left-over money for some chips and a bag of beers. Sometimes, just sometimes, it's a lucky day. Now if only we could have had the three points as well!

We have done this for years. We always worked out that if you requested assistance, i.e. a ramp, the staff were too lazy or disorganised to facilitate this. So, you would sit around for ten minutes then go to customer services and moan a bit. All you had to say was that you are stranded as we had missed our Dial a Ride. They would arrange a free taxi home, now from Euston you are looking at £25 so for me and my brother that's a bullseye, so straight back to the ruby house then home with the money saved. Sometimes we would say we were so angry that we needed to calm down and could they get the taxi to pick us up from the Royal George pub opposite Euston.

I am sure people will say we took the piss, and yep, to an extent we did. People will say fares will go up and share prices will go down. Really, from the few quid a few skint working-class blokes saved, it wouldn't even touch the chief executive's bonus. People often say to me "You turn your disability into an advantage" and why they say this negatively, I don't know. I have never been a 'poor me' or 'the world owes me a living' type due to my disability. Society and the world in general cannot deal with any criticism regarding so-called marginalised groups, whether it's ethics, disabled, gay, Muslim, you name it. All terms society isn't comfortable with. Big companies don't want the stigma and sadly, they have created monsters.

But if I can turn something into my advantage then too fucking right I will.

With booze and a few lads out for the day, things could sometimes get a little messy. Some days following the Lions just seemed to raise the bar in silliness and you can always tell when people go too far and cross the line. Terms like 'in high jinks' and 'enjoying the moment' come out. It's just a polite way of saying they don't give a fuck.

One such game was a visit to see us at Crewe Alexander. All I know about Crewe is that it's full of pervy train spotters; it's one of the answers when people ask you to name five league football teams with an X in the name and finally, it holds the memory of a pit stop on the way to Wigan in a playoff game with me entering a pub with a photograph of Bobby Moore on the wall which my dad took outside and destroyed.

We arrived early, about 20 of us, and were all out to have a great day, have a booze and collect a rare three points on our travels. We went straight into the first pub we saw. That's what I love about Millwall, as, when you get off a train in a town you don't know, more so in a rough town, some teams will wait to be taken to a pub en-route to the ground. Millwall just march into the first pub they see and don't care about who it's allocated to. Does it serve beer? Yep, we're going in. After sinking a few in the pub and kick off hours away, the talk turns to birds. One of the boys says, "*I was working up here a few months back, there is a superb massage parlour two minutes from this pub*". Everyone starts shouting out and giving him stick or saying what they would like to do there. I kept a bit quiet and started finding out how far the place was and if I would get in. It seemed that it was

156

a five-minute walk, so boom, I was having that. I went around with two mates and within a few minutes and a lot of cash lighter I was having the time of my life. I came out with a pair of Alan Wickers (Alan Wickers = knickers) in my hand and chucked them at my pal as we entered the pub which had roast potatoes on the bar for us; I love that northern hospitality.

We went over to the game and by now the knickers had been placed on my head. Think Wyatt and Gary in Weird Science with the bras on their heads. I must have looked a right oddball, but my mates still nicked them to put them on though. At one point the Millwall striker Ben May who, to be honest, was crap, and believed he was better than us, got gobby with the Millwall fans. I'm screaming and shouting with a beer inside me with stewards, police, even a few players looking at me, thinking is this bloke in the chair for real with the knickers on his head? It's a shame or maybe not, that we didn't have camera telephones in those days.

It wasn't always me who played the silly boy and I remember going to see Millwall at Deans Court just before Christmas in 1996. It was freezing cold and it was the old Deans Court before it had graced the Premiership. I was plonked on the terraces to warm up and sober up and just before half time we walked to the food kiosk; well, I say kiosk, but it was a hole in the wall. My pal asked me what I wanted. "Anything that looks like it won't give me food poisoning" and he passed me a horrible looking burger. He then began passing food to the person behind me and I presumed he was being helpful. Then the next person received a coffee and sausage roll as random strangers were receiving random food gifts. The kiosk guy told me and my pal to return to our plot and about five minutes later I noticed some police talking to the kiosk staff. Within a few minutes they were in front of us asking us to pay the £210 we owed for food. I quickly pointed out it was nothing to do with us, but the problem the police had was that they knew the score, but didn't want to wind up the fans. My pal stated he was only trying to help people get served. To our amazement the police returned to the kiosk staff to inform them that not much was happening. I suppose now as a Premiership team that £200 is not even an assist bonus, but a few years after our trip, the Cherries fell on hard times, and we always wound my friend up that he could've been the nail in their coffin.

Going to Millwall has given me the opportunity to see some of my generation's greatest English players in the flesh. Lineker, Gascoigne, Paul Scholes, Gary Neville (both in an FA Cup Final), Seaman, Shilton, Glen Hoddle, and Ian Wright. You can add a bit of stardust with Karl-Heinz Rummenigge and Christiano Ronaldo, and, it may not seem a lot to you, but to a football fan who has spent his life in the lower leagues, there are some greats there. But they will never be held in the esteem that Rae, Lovell, Harris, Stevens, Keller, Hurlock, Cahill, Kevin Bremner (Google him, one of my first footballing heroes), Morison, Thatcher and the Lord himself, Cascarino, are held.

I thank my lucky stars that the best thing my dad ever did was to get us down The Den and into football. Football is the biggest ice breaker, and starting a new job or meeting the in-laws for the first time, if you find they are a football supporter you have something to talk about. My father-in-law is a Millwall fan too, so our first meeting went well and my initial fears were unwarranted, but the best thing about supporting Millwall is you know you are guaranteed a ticket if they play a big game. I have had a season ticket since my teenage years and all my friends have memberships, so, in the unlikely event of Manchester United away in the FA Cup we are guaranteed a ticket. I would love to see Millwall in the Premiership for one season just so we can visit the so-called elite. We would be like the family member who no-one likes at parties. We would turn up and not give a monkey's...

The Club and the people who run it frustrate me immensely. They seem obsessed with changing our fan base and this isn't unique to Millwall. Accept our fans for what and who we are, and of course you can't produce official merchandise praising our fans for exploits off the pitch, but they should maintain an identity and never conform. The other side of the coin is the love and support I have received from the club at my most difficult times. Not all Millwall fans are thugs; far from it; the media want you to believe they are, but they are not. They are working-class people who will always have a different mindset. I am proud of my working-class roots and attribute most of my success in dealing with my condition to these roots. Millwall fans are good people and you will not find a more loyal and generous group. These so-called hooligans are the people who have treated me so well during my time following football, but I acknowledge that standards have slipped. This is because we have a new generation of fans who don't understand what being a football fan and more importantly a Millwall fan, is all about. They will have watched Green Street and The Football Factory, but this is society's problem, not Millwall's.

The club to this day still drives me mad. People will be banned for the most stupid things as the desire to be seen to be 'doing the right thing' is so high. But after all my moans about the club, I have to say that when things have been desperate for me, they have always shown support, like when my brother died. They went out of their way to ensure his funeral cortege passed through The Den and when we stopped, they came out of the office and placed a signed pennant on his coffin. When I was in hospital recovering from Swine Flu and having a tracheostomy, they wrote to me with a get well soon letter signed by the entire team and an invite to a VIP Day out once I was better. This spurred me on so much. But the biggest was the support they showed when my mum passed away. We wanted her wake at Millwall and a true gent called Mark Cole moved heaven and earth to rearrange bookings they had already made. You don't forget these things. In 2022 when I was told I wouldn't be leaving hospital and was coming to the end of my journey, it was Millwall fans and the club itself who stepped in to support my family and my young son, making him mascot at Watford away on Boxing Day.

Millwall are constantly abused in the media and while I agree with the 'give a dog a bad name' rationale I am also able to acknowledge that we do probably deserve some of the stick. Yet much worse goes on up and down the country on a weekly basis, but everyone knows us and it's not because of our on-field achievements. The inconsistencies of the media's reporting of incidents involving Millwall are bizarre, unjustified and stink of a hidden agenda.

Some of you reading this will think if the fans didn't misbehave then there wouldn't be a problem and you're a 100% correct, but the double standards are there for all to see. I've stated many times in this book that we deserve all we get, yet the protecting of the Premiership where racism, bottle throwing and anti-social behaviour is more widespread is overlooked, swept under the carpet and pushed aside. Why? Because money talks and the brand has to be protected. It's a circus and deserves to be treated as such.

On the other side of the coin, our fans will moan about the stick we receive from the authorities and media, yet not acknowledge that for the best part of fifty years we have stuck two fingers up to everyone and anyone.

We sing *'No one likes us, we don't care'* for a reason and that's how I like it.

CAT IN THE CRADLE

You're probably wondering who we are going to discuss here and it can only be one person. My dad, Dennis, but we call him the Duke.

My dad has always been a hard worker but also a ducker and diver, he will believe everyone is on a fiddle and more importantly, that they are entitled to be. When he had one of the only periods of being out of work, I tried hard while working in the Jobcentre to look out for employment for him. I would often telephone him to inform him of a job and the reply was always "What's it involve?" Now as fair a question as that may sound, if it was delivering fruit 'n veg, he would turn his nose up, but if I had said meat, the pound note signs in his head would roll as he thought of those fillet steaks he could sell to his pals.

My mum met my dad in a pub near Lambeth North tube station called The Hercules, and why she didn't hear the alarm bells on that first meeting, only she knows. He was there with a few mates and was paid to go around local pubs to cause a fight; the bouncers would then chuck them out and have a valid case to protect the pub. My dad would then get 'a drink' from the bloke who organised the doors and arrangements like this have been the corner stone of my old man's life.

My dad has always been physically tough and growing up you always felt safe. I have been in many tight squeezes where the odds have been against us, but my dad's ability to hold his own and show he meant business turned things around. He was never a bully and I have never seen him physically start on someone.

I've talked loads about his Millwall exploits but even today, some 40 years on, I will get people say 'You're Dennis Evans' boy. Your dad could look after himself". He has taught me some good life skills at a young age, with the main one being you don't need to look for trouble; if you want trouble it will come and find you. He also told me that people who tell you they have never lost a row are full of bullshit and no matter who you are you will take a pasting one or two times in ten. I remember as kids he went to Fratton Park to see Millwall play. On a suicide mission he went into the home end with his friend Dedge and within seconds the punches were coming in, Dad was on the floor and kicked unconscious. He made it home the next day black and blue.

I suppose my dad was your normal bloke in the 70's; probably got married too young and was hard-working, but was still craving those weekends with his mates. But he was married now, with two kids, and it was time to step up to the plate. He would show glimpses of being able to do it, but would always end up back down The Den and on the beer before and after.

Once me and Dames were diagnosed with Muscular Dystrophy, things should have changed, he should have knuckled down more. Maybe in his eyes he did, and maybe he tried harder, but he never reached the level needed. I remember going to hospital appointments as a kid and, yes, he attended some, but he missed more. I can still see the 2.4 families with the dad being the head and dealing with it all, but that was never going to be us. I probably wouldn't have wanted that either, and in my mum, we had someone who led from the front so no one else was needed.

I think too many people have been quick to be judgemental about my dad over the years as he has done some horrendous things and some that I am shocked we have managed to come back from, but if me, my mum and Ginge could, then surely others should respect that. But of course, they were only watching out for us and we are lucky to have had that support.

But can you imagine what it must have been like for the Duke? He has these two boys and he would have had dreams for us, but they would have been snatched away by an illness no one seems to understand now, let alone forty years ago. My heart goes out to him and maybe I understand things better now I'm a dad too.

It is still all so raw. I remember as a kid going to a football training event Millwall had put on. That old donkey, later to be England Manager and dodgy bloke Sam Allardyce was training the kids.

As a kid I remember wanting to attend a Millwall football trial. I was eight and could hardly walk, let alone play football, but I still wanted to do it. It was at a school near Millwall and it was just a chance for kids to have a kick about in front of coaches from Millwall and a few players. In the end my dad relented and took me to "watch". After half an hour he spotted a few mates so went over for a chat. I'm pretty sure my pals Jodie and Jamie were playing on one of the pitches as they have always been excellent footballers in our circle.

I was watching the game just standing there and one of the coaches asked me to join. Boom, I was straight on the pitch only to be knocked flying in minutes. I'm laid out on the gravel and trying so hard not to cry, but the next thing I'm being lifted up by a giant with a big tash. Low and behold it was the Millwall defender Sam Allardyce, who said in a strong northern accent *"Come on son, let's get you out of harm's way"*. I was star struck and that star could join the ones in my head after the knock I had. My dad then comes running over and takes me off Big Sam who then continues to talk football with him. Cool story and name drop there, but to be rescued by a future England Manager, wow. Afterwards my dad was upset. He sensed the difference between me and the rest of the kids but he didn't love me any less, he just struggled to find that "niche market" where he could accept what we could do. As me and Ginge become adults it become a lot easier for him but he still struggles today. He is so proud of what I have achieved. I look on it and play it down on the whole. I've got a beautiful wife, an amazing boy who I adore and a nice house. I get to all the football and cricket matches I want to and I do as much as my peers, and that's what matters to me.

I jumped in with all my dad's mates' kids and within seconds I was knocked to the floor. Dad was over the fence lifting me up and carrying me back, but was in tears as he was doing it. He had all the compassion a dad should have and he was surrounded by mates telling him not to get upset, but he just could not take on our condition. People who criticise him should step back and think how they would cope. Bollock him for the balls up he has made, too right, but not for not being able to deal with the situation. I decided a long time ago that my dad deserves a break with how he dealt with our situation, it was far from ideal but it is what it is and the achievement is we are still close and have a healthy relationship. The key is not to confuse the understanding of how he felt about a demanding and unique situation with that of Dennis being Dennis and out for a beer and laugh. I allow myself to make that judgement as it was myself and Ginge who've gone through it and had to stomach it. Like many 80's and 90's dads, he just never grew up; even in the new version of him I can still go weeks without contact.

My dad just went missing so many times. As a kid I just couldn't understand it and thought we had done something wrong. Even now I still struggle to understand it. He would go early one morning for work and not be seen for a few weeks. These disappearing acts become longer and more frequent. Life chucks up some incredible challenges and is not a Hollywood film with the characters who can solve everything. It is about humans and maybe he just needed a breather from the daily struggle. But this was a luxury my mum didn't have.

Up until my teens we went through the same dad drinking too much, getting into trouble at work or football and the 'I'm a changed man' routine. But some of the scrapes were funny, looking back. He had to work until mid-day on a Saturday. He would be out by 10.30am and in a pub in New Cross by 11.30am if Millwall were at home, but if we were away, he would be out at 9.30am at the latest.

One day he didn't get his usual luck finish and I think he got out around 1pm. Millwall were away to someone like Walsall so he was never going to make the game. Did he rush home to take us

166

down the park? Nope, he went straight to the BBC Social Club for a session and to watch the results come in. At around 4.45pm when the usual defeat for Millwall came in, and for reasons best known only to him, he decided to chuck the television at the window. Now he must have forgotten the bar was on the 5th floor of the Television Centre on Wood Lane and after the television exploded on to the floor below, he was escorted off the premises by security but, somehow, he managed to avoid both arrest and dismissal. He was lucky that somewhere in the organisation he worked for was a bleeding-heart liberal calling the shots who felt sorry for the working-class fella with two disabled kids. Maybe it was the start of the BBC that drives me so mad today.

How did my mum put up with all this? Well, there were obviously some amazing times and we had some great holidays with so many funny times as my dad is extremely witty and sharp. When he was really bad, my mum would call on his dad, Grandad George, to have a word. I literally hung on every word my grandad said and, the times he did have to come, he was a hero coming to save the day in my eyes. I suppose my dad was just doing what most blokes do in their late 30's when confronted by their angry dad, just listen and say the right things, but knowing they just want to get out and get back on the booze.

Long before my back operation in 1990, my dad had left home and both my parents kept up the 'working away' story, but kids are more clued up than people give them credit for. When I came out of the hospital in pain I was now promoted to 'Man of the House' which was a job I never wanted or was capable of, but would still have a go at doing it.

After a few years, things settled down and dad become more stable in our lives. For all that has gone on, I wouldn't change him for the world as you get one mum and one dad, so cherish them. I just hope Jude feels the same about me! I still get a buzz out of seeing him and he still has the same hard luck stories he has peddled for forty years to me with the same excuses for being late. But I wouldn't change him for the world. We have a weird relationship but one I cherish, and a pint with him on our own is priceless. I always find my dad good company, especially if it just us two, and over the years we have overcome some sad times. We have also worked on having a healthy relationship and staying in contact, which is not easy when you are a bit hot-headed like me and have someone like my dad who seems to be going in the opposite direction as you. That could be anything. The things that wind him up I laugh at or accept, but it is vice versa, as he can't understand my ridged mentality.

Even now my dad can't really cope with my condition. If I'm in hospital and about to have a blood test or my trach changed, he will say "Do you want me to pop to the shop mate?" and I will tell him to wait, but by the time I turn around he is outside having a cigarette. I laugh. I don't think any worse of him as it's how he deals with things. Sadly, Muscular Dystrophy will always be a massive focal point of our relationship, only because he just can't handle what it has done to myself and Ginge, but can you blame him? It's nicked one son from him and will take his other too.

I know my dad is very proud of me and what I have achieved and that makes me happy. To see him with Jude just takes away all the silliness we have been through and he is so patient, much more than when we were kids. I suppose many grandads are like this. Jude loves him as he has that silly way that kids love from adults, and seeing them bonding together makes me very happy. So, he is Peter Pan; he may have been for many years, all through his 40's and 50's. I mean the amount of time someone would march up to me in a pub and go *"Have a word with your dad,"* it was like I was the adult. Maybe, just maybe, he is starting to mature.

I have always loved my dad. To be honest I think that's half my problem as I have always wanted and needed more from him; there are millions of kids who have grown up like this. After my mum died, I certainly expected more from him, which was probably unrealistic, but to think after all that, all the MD talk. I'm in my 40s and still that little boy who loved being carried up the steps at Cold Blow Lane by Gentle Ben, his dad who everyone seemed to know. That is a memory of happiness that will live with me forever and no one will take that away. So, after all the ups and downs we still have something.

YOU CAN'T HURRY LOVE

Many people write about their life and include exploits of their sexual conquests and how many women they have had the pleasure of taking to bed. Sadly, I am not in a position to do that, well definitely not for the first years of adulthood, but I did make up for it in my late 20's.

I was absolutely useless with birds. In my early 20's I just couldn't work out why I wasn't getting any 'Satisfaction' as Mick the Lips would say.

I wasn't Brad Pitt, but not ugly either, and I was always well groomed. I could hold a half sensible conversation and was generous, but most of all I was a gentleman. All this has been confirmed to me by numerous people from both sexes in the past. No, not by my nan, but by many trusted friends who wouldn't just say things for the sake of making me feel better. At times I seemed to resemble a male Bridget Jones, anything that could go wrong around meeting girls would go wrong, it seemed. The stories in this chapter shaped me; there's some that I reflect on and think blimey, that's harsh, but there's nothing I'm ashamed off. I'm proud I stuck at it, none of it was perfect, but then again, my deck of cards in life wasn't. It was about stumbling through it.

If you're reading this today and have Duchenne's, you can do it too. You'll get there. Honestly there's someone for everyone out there. Today's Duchenne lads have a different challenge. The fake Social Media world and online dating must be their answer to a brass house in Balham when it comes to getting experience.

I laugh and think I've had a lucky escape when people tell me about websites like Tinder and how often they just get a random bunk up. I'm glad it wasn't about when I was young, I'd have killed myself with an over sexed induced heart attack as it seems it's a free for all. The following stories will show learning curves. Like everyone else, the curve just lasted a lot longer than most.

I went to all the usual Meat Markets to meet the girls. Caesars in Old Kent Road was my favourite. While I did have one or two moments of success in there, it was never the Promised Land it should have been. Women were literally giving it away like it was going out of fashion, but I always ended up with the rough, nasty borderline psychopath out of a group of four or five. My mates would go steaming onto the nice ones leaving me with the moany one who didn't want to be there or just wanted a punch up. One was a girl we christened the 'Little Old Lady who lived in the Shoe'. Well, if you know the rest of the nursery rhyme, you will know why we called her that.

At 19 she had four kids by four different blokes and I often spent hours at my desk on a Monday trying to work out the maths and how she fitted them all in. She was a nice enough girl, but after a few visits to her flat and having kids' toys launched at my head and Heinz baby food dropped over my rhythms (rhythms and blues = shoes) I decided to cut my losses and call it a day.

I was in Caesars once and a mate said *"I think the bird round there fancies you"*. Boom, I was all ears and he went off to get her. When he came back, I just presumed he was on a wind up as he was on his own. Well actually he wasn't, I just hadn't seen the midget walking alongside him. She was another odd one and seemed to be off her head on something. Well, she jumped up onto my lap which seemed to have most of the club in tears of laughter. I stayed and spoke to her for a bit, but needed a piss. But as there were no disabled toilets, my mate pushed me outside to the alleyway at the side. Just as I was about to come back in, the midget appeared, so I sent my mate back in and spent a bit of time getting to know her outside! It was freezing out there and I came inside to a few cheers from my mates. Luckily on this night there was only a few of us out.

The next morning Millwall had an away game. We were waiting in the Walworth Road really early for taxis, and me and my pal were rough from the night before. As we stood there on the cold road side which is similar to a High Street, I could see someone waving from the top deck of the bus. It was only the poxy midget! For fuck's sake, how unlucky am I? She must be local so I tried to wave politely but discreetly. One of my pals was going *"Who's the bird?"* and straight away my mate goes *"Oh she's the midget Lee copped hold of in Caesars last night"*. Struggling to put a slant on it, I noticed her getting off the bus all three feet five inches of her and she came straight over to start chatting. I know how to converse confidently in most if not all situations, but this was a challenging and awkward few minutes. It wasn't her disability that was causing me to be hot under the collar, I mean nobody is more broken than me. It was just that classic awkward next day chance encounter but finally she left and I spent the rest of the day being ripped apart.

So, the little old woman who lived in the shoe and the midget were about as good as it got for 6 years.

After years of not getting anywhere amazing with the birds I suddenly found some success in my late 20's. Up until then it had been a ratio of getting a bit once every 6 months. On one long drought I went a year without getting any at all. Now don't get me wrong I didn't get it down to a weekly thing, but I got it down to at least monthly. By now the whole I can't accept any *"sympathy votes"* as my mates called them, had long gone. If a girl felt sorry for me then I would usually accept anything she was going to offer me. Don't look a gift horse in the mouth. Come on, be fair, would you?

After losing my virginity at 19 to an encounter that lasted minutes in the college disabled toilet, it was pretty hit and miss for the early twenties of my life. On the odd occasions I did get something, I was like the cat that had got the cream around my pals. What changed? First of all, I worked out square pegs and round holes (no innuendo there) and up until my mid to late 20s I was trying to pull the young fit birds in night clubs. Nothing wrong with that, but I seemed to have to put a lot more effort in for a lot less success. They were also high maintenance and I wanted the quick fix. By chance I discovered the single mum's; girls in their late 20's to early 30's who get one night out a month and wanted to enjoy it. They want to have a good drink and a laugh. I have always been a good talker and been able to crack a joke, so straight away so I had half a chance. At the end of the night, they wanted a bit of a laugh and to get home by breakfast before their babysitter was up.

I found this target group by chance. Once I had recognised my target audience, I found I was lucky enough to live in an area that had them by the thousands, and the local Housing Estates were full of them. I think I have done more for the single women of Southwark than Working Families Tax Credit. Some passed through the door once, but quite a few I would see again, or better still stayed in contact with. It was easy, they didn't expect anything from you with no commitment, because they couldn't give you one back. But they accepted me at face value and that's what I had been crying out for over the last decade. This may sound a bit shallow, but it worked for everyone. It's happening a thousand times every weekend up and down the country but for me it was my Eureka moment.

Work then became a major player in my pulling and I try to be a nice bloke in life. Yep, I'm hard work at times but only when I have to stand my ground. Working in a Jobcentre you can deal with negative situations, but if you speak politely and people believe you are helping them, they will normally warm to you. I wasn't one of those leechy blokes perving. I just tried to be helpful and before you knew it, people were on good terms with you. The department I worked for had a strict policy on friendships in the workplace but come on, I've never done anything illegal or corrupt, far from being a jobsworth, I just didn't need the extra hassle. Also, as I was contributing to our mortgage, I couldn't risk losing my job.

But as time went on, I met so many nice people from all walks of life, but it was the women I enjoyed meeting the most. A French girl came in looking for work and was about four years older than me. I helped her find a part time job in a restaurant in

Camberwell. I would meet her every Friday outside Iceland on Walworth Road as it was a good landmark and near both of us and I would use the dentist excuse to get out of work. I hadn't been to the dentist in twenty odd years but my work must have thought I was Jaws from James Bond.

The first few times we met it was just for a coffee and a chat, and like most blokes, I knew when I was in with a chance, I just needed to play the game. After a few weeks of meeting on a Friday, we were just going straight to mine for *"a bit"* in the afternoon.

I also met a really attractive girl from the Ukraine. In the end though, as pretty as she was, she drove me mad as all she ever did was slag off England. *"The weather is crap"*. Well ok but it's about -15 where you're from love. *"I don't like the food here"*. I do and at least we don't have to queue two weeks for a loaf of bread love. So that was never really going to last, I tried hard to be the diplomat but after constant criticism of our country I had to hit back.

The final "work experience" is one that many people frown upon but my whole life mantra is about being honest about myself. On a trip to Amsterdam, like many young blokes, I discovered the Red Light District. Nothing shocking about that, but in my late 20's a visit to the Dam became my second hobby after Millwall. I was always there; it was like a home from home. It seemed like I was there every couple of months. You will get some women go *"you dirty bastard"*. For me it is a vice in the same league as drink, drugs or gambling. What a young single bloke down the road gets up to isn't really front-page news is it, as it was all safe and above board.

175

I remember being out in Amsterdam with about fifteen pals. On the Saturday we were smashed and a few of us got split up, so our group had about four of us in it. We walked past a window and it had this stunning blonde girl in it and my pal said *"Do you fancy a go?"* Well, it would have been rude not to, so I sent him off to broker the deal. When he came back, he was mumbling about her being a bit odd, but I presumed he meant she was a bit snappy or something. As soon as I went in she just switched on me. She was in thigh high leather boots and a tight leather bra with studs and had a whip that must have been two feet long and she was more useful with it than Indiana Jones. I started trying to tell her to stop but she wasn't having any of it. She was in full act and was a better method actor than Daniel Day Lewis. She was ripping my shirt open and the whip was literally brushing my ears as it went past. I was shit scared and begging to be let out. She then went even weirder and mumbled about I had paid for twenty minutes so I must stay, so she sat down on a chair and started sticking Kit Kats inside herself and then in my mouth. My mates heard me shouting and banged on the door.

Like a light switch being turned off she went all normal and said, *"Let me get your friends"* and *"Why didn't you say the safe word if you wanted me to stop? I told your friend to tell you it"*. I walked out with a ripped shirt, red marks from a whip on my face and covered in melted chocolate. My mates were in tears, my brother was slaughtering me, and by the time I was home I was christened Kit Kat and forever having them chucked at me. I would be at the pub or Millwall and a Kit Kat would come flying at me, *"Have that you perv!"*

I was in Amsterdam once on a nice summer's evening when me and my pal were standing outside a window. My mate ran off to get some beers to quench our thirst while I got speaking to a big group of German lads on a stag weekend. I think for some reason they thought I was a virgin and had some pity for me. One of them made the suggestion that they would treat me to one of the girls in the window out of their whip money. How could I ever turn that offer down?

I was carried up the steps in the chair by these friendly Germans and when I came out after my time was up, I was greeted to a loud cheer from the group. My response was to wave like one of the Beatles when they landed on their first trip to America. I think the phrase needed was Danke.

On the few times I tried to access adult services in London, it always led to some odd results and would never have me accessing the services I was looking for. These stories would later have us all laughing.

My good friend Dunphy is a Millwall fan and close family friend, and I would end up marrying his cousin Kellie. Now Dunphy, like most Irish (he is from Walworth but like a lot of second-generation House Bricks (House Bricks = Micks), has that annoying habit of wanting to be Irish), loves a beer, and to make it worse his parents own a pub, so he is constantly pissed. We would always be out after Millwall on the beer. He is a labourer and works all over London and about 3am one morning we were in a pub talking about brothels. Dunphy was telling us he had seen one near a job in Hoxton he was working on, so forty-five minutes later me, Dunphy and a pal were in a taxi en-route to Hoxton. It was a summer's night but at that time the temperature had dropped and I remember us all being in shorts and feeling the cold. Once there, Dunphy was marching ahead through a maze of backstreets and we were struggling to keep up with him. He then disappeared into a doorway and as we caught him up, he was eager to get in with his usual tactic of me paying. *"The bloke in the chair will pay"* as he slipped through the double doors. At that point me and my pal couldn't help but notice the number of men in tight pants and with a rolled-up towel heading towards the doors Dunphy had gone through. We had twigged it was a gay sauna.

Like Sun journalists we made our excuses and left and about 30 seconds later a rather shocked Dunphy came running down to catch us up. Now thirty seconds is a long time when you are scared, but I'm still wondering why it took him so long to get out of there. Once he calmed down he said it was just groups of men having a mass orgy, a real free for all.

Another balls up on our quest to find a high-class brothel was helped by some intel from someone who I always knew was a wally, but on this occasion my pal convinced me the bloke knew his stuff. We wanted a place that was classy and had probably watched too many films and these places I doubt even existed in South East London. *"Head to Sydenham, we were told. It will cost you a monkey lad, but this place is high class"*. I was well up for it. Now Sydenham is quite posh, not all of it, but some of it, and tucked behind the old Crystal Palace you have Lawrie Park, an area that was owned by the Lawrie family many years ago.

My pal told the cabbie to head to Lawrie Park in Sydenham and I presumed he knew exactly where, as in Lawrie Park there is Lawrie Park Road, Lawrie Park Avenue, Lawrie Park Crescent and

Lawrie Park Gardens. Now my pissed-up pal armed with the door number and Lawrie Park is on a mission to find these women we had been promised. I kept asking him if he knew where we were going and he would mutter a door number. By now we are out of the cab and walking around and he clocks these houses he believes to be our goal. Pukka house, massive drive, a few nice cars on the drive. As we walked in my wheelchair made so much noise with the gravel on the drive. My pal is pressing the doorbell and is now banging on the door a bit impatiently. Next thing we have heard a commotion upstairs. Some bloke has put his head out of the window *"What do you want?"* he snapped. My pal is all laid back *"Come down fella and let us in"*. The bloke is arguing with him, then a woman in her 40's appears, my mate goes to me *"I don't think much of yours, the sorts must be in the swimming pool"*.

Then the bloke from inside is now at the door but with the chain on, and goes *"What address do you want?"* and I can hear my pal talking and rather sheepishly going *"Oh right, so Lawrie Park Avenue is the next one, sorry pal"*. He sticks his chest out, shoulders high and kicks the brakes off the wheelchair. We walked out across the noisy chippings like it was Downton Abbey and once outside he goes *"I've got the wrong fucking street, mate"*.

Nowadays, you will have a very high percentage of young lads between 20-35 just going away and getting a bit. You can say otherwise, but it's fact, as this is the modern world we live in. People just want everything on the move, less commitment to the old world. You then get bored of it all and meet someone special and think shit, I've wasted a long time mucking around.

But maybe you need to get all of this out of your system before you do settle down. I know so many blokes who married too young. My dad is a prime example; he needed to get out and about until his 30's.

So, for a few years before I met Kellie my success improved.

I learnt the skill of playing my cards close to my chest. If I liked someone then I would talk and get to know them. I never got in the habit of talking about girls I liked, as I found that a waste of time. Throughout this period of doing well, of course my condition would have to affect my plans. It could be from coming down ill with a chest infection hours before a date or planning a night in and a carer to come at 11pm to get you on the bed, only for the carer to telephone in sick and you end up having to be on the bed for 6pm.

One occasion, that sticks out as an awkward jubilee moment during my prosperous period, came after I got to know a girl who worked for Marks and Spencer on Walworth Road and who would often drink in our local pub, Liam Ogs, after she had finished work. Let's call her Sally. Now Sally was a big old unit, very pretty and was a nice girl. I had got to know her through the pub, we had gone on to meet up a for a few midweek drinks, these led to a grabbed takeaway on our way back to mine, a bit of nookie and bang she was up at 5am to get back to Marks and Spencer to put the soft white Farmhouse loaves and Chocolate Éclairs out for the morning rush. Me, well I would stay in bed for a few hours before wandering into the Jobcentre after the early giro issue.

Now my mates have always been obsessed with me having sex in my overhead hoist. I'd like to point out I have never had sex in my overhead hoist. It was something my mates spent far too much time going on about. It was forever mentioned on a lad's night out *"I bet you'd like to get her in your hoist"* and the favourite *"You'd wear the battery out taking her up and down"*. It was then renamed by my friends as the sex swing.

One night we were all out, a few of us, and Sally was out with a mate. One of the boys said something funny about the hoist quietly, but it was obviously not quiet enough, as on the walk home that night Sally asked about the hoist. I laughed and told her what the boys always said. She found it funny and that seemed to be the end of the chat, but a week or so later she mentioned it again and then again. One night on the walk home she actually asked if she could get in the hoist while we had sex. I presumed it was a joke but I quickly understood she was serious, so I said yes straight away, mainly because I didn't want to piss her off and give up regular nights out, sex and the reduced rib eye steaks she was getting me from work. Also, I'm one of those in for a penny in for a pound people, why not, eh?

As we got nearer home, I did start to worry. The hoist had a weight limit of 200kg. Now whilst Sally was big, she was nowhere near that weight but I was thinking how far out are we here? We're home in bed and she's dangling about 2ft off my waist. She's also swinging from side to side and I'm trying to guide her down whilst she is fumbling with the hoist control. The nearest thing I can compare it to is one of those arcade machines where you have a grabber to help you win an unwinnable prize. If I'm honest, I was getting the hump already.

She was laughing and as she's coming down, she chucks the control over her head, even today I'm not sure why she did that, but if the aim was to fuck, we're now completely fucked as her legs are resting on my legs and neither of us can reach the remote control. What are we going to do? She hasn't got a Danny (Danny La Rue = clue). I can't call my mum who's upstairs, can I? Equally though, we've got to solve this before she comes down in the morning to see me. Sally starts to swing back and forth to get some momentum to move up in the sling to reach the hoist control. This was a good idea to be fair, but the only issue being that as she swung, her legs were hitting my body and a fair bit of damage was being done. It felt like I was getting a good old-fashioned kicking. This went on for what seemed like hours, but was more like six or seven minutes and when she finally grabbed the remote, the euphoria from both of us was greater than all of our previous nights put together. As we both collapsed onto the bed, I thought fuck, never again am I doing that. We went to sleep pretty quickly.

Things drifted apart pretty quickly after that night. Whilst I missed the free Joe (Joe Blake = steak) I was pretty much relieved. I didn't say much to the boys for a few weeks, mainly as I didn't want them to take the piss out of Sally if she was in the pub. But boy when I finally told them they had tears running down their faces.

After traveling the journey of love I've mentioned above, I would be lying if I said my condition hadn't made an impact on my ability to form close loving relationships with women in my younger years. I have passed the opinion that it probably did me good in later life that I had lived a bit of a varied life. In fairness I would say the problem was just as much about my own confidence as well as negative stances from the ones I chased.

People who know me will struggle to believe that I had confidence issues around women as I just thought why would they want me when they can have someone who's legs work? Luckily in my late 20's maturity kicked in and I started to understand the world and how it worked. More, being physically perfect isn't an optimum attribute for so many, being kind and graceful is though. I started to believe in myself a bit more, in fact a lot more. While I was never over the top and cock-sure, I found some inner belief; the catalyst to powering this belief was I just looked around one night and thought you've never given up on anything else in life so why are you giving up now?

For a bloke with a lot of obstacles in front of him, I've done well. We would always say as a group of lads I can drink as much as you, go to Millwall as much as you and pull as much as you. It may sound silly but to young lads in a group that's all that matters.

DON'T LOOK BACK IN ANGER

Dames, Ginger, or Ginge to those who were close to him, is my benchmark in life. Everything I do I compare it to him and the high standards he set, but sometimes I feel I have fallen short and that can upset me. Most siblings have the elder as the leader and I was the front man for the band as I made the big speeches which got the troops rallied for any big day out, but when it mattered it was Ginge people listened to. I've seen him at age 23 advising people in their mid-forties. He wasn't a know it all and wouldn't get involved in other people's business, but if you sought his advice you knew whatever you told him went no further.

His condition, or our condition, always seemed to affect him more. At the time, it was happening in front of me and I never understood how lucky I was to be in a better situation. Like two bald men fighting over a comb, neither of us seemed to notice the comparisons between the individuality of our condition. Sometimes it was obvious to see. One example while slipping into my Stone Islands and slapping on the Armani aftershave before I went out, Ginge was laying on the bed next door struggling to breathe.

Now, these days I'm lost. I feel I've lost my point of reference. Selfishly did Ginge being worse push me on? Probably, but I always had a drive to stay healthy to support him.

Now when my health is bad, I'm a mess, and my doctors tell me not to compare myself to Ginge as I'm different, but who else do

I have to compare myself with? I'm totally shit at mixing with disabled people, especially ones with Muscular Dystrophy. Why you ask? I don't actually know. There is a part that they bore me as all they want to do is talk about the condition and its effects. Yes, if you're calling me arrogant, hard work, in denial, I'm probably all of them on this subject and Ginge was the same. I mean I make a token effort when people talk to me, but Ginge would just look ahead and ignore them. He had enough problems of his own he would say, and he wasn't asking anyone to help him with his, so don't expect him to understand for others what he couldn't understand himself. Cor, harsh and cold, and I do get it, but my mum would go mad at him. She would help anyone and would tell him to stop being rude, but he would say "you go and chat with them then", which most times she did. Now I just sit there in hospital looking at the walls thinking of the shit Ginge went through and how I ain't really got a clue what's happening to me, and I'm relieved. Too much information is dangerous.

If my brother was alive today, he would be plotted up in a council flat off the Walworth Road with a Mrs running around after him and a kid, I reckon. He always had birds and I don't know how, as he hardly went anywhere. When he did you knew he was going to make it count and he had them tucked all over the place. Me, oh, I was proper moody about it. He would bring home the bacon, a right little sort, and after a few weeks you would have all the family going *"We've met Lucy. Now when are you going to get a young lady, Lee?"*

He had it hard though, my brother, always did. I remember as kids him always falling and hurting himself. Playing football in the school hall while my mum was working as a cleaner, he fell and hit his head on the corner of the wall. He ended up splitting his canister open and needing 60 odd stitches; he was only a young 'un of about 8. I also remember going to Portugal on holiday as a kid. While we were in a bar, I heard a big crash and commotion. Next thing my dad had run over to see Ginge had fallen over and smashed his head open. The bar owners had called an ambulance and my dad and Uncle Bill had to take him to hospital to have his head stitched up. We also did a sponsored walk for Muscular Dystrophy all around the City of London one weekend. Ginge fell over, done all his face in, and needed stitches after the wheelchair hit a broken pavement.

Ginge had a reputation of being a bit shrewd around a pound note and was only about ten when he wrote to the bank who had the pavement outside their office. He argued for months, then started talking about the legal aspects and contacting the media so they asked him to drop it all for just shy of a grand. Not bad for a young kid and I never saw much of it. That was Dames all over, using his brain where most would just let it go. He could have done anything he wanted. I think motivation and losing a lot of confidence as a kid made him lose interest in things. He still achieved so much though.

Once the whole Muscular Dystrophy thing kicked in it was heart-breaking. Seeing your brother who was a lump as a kid go down to under five stone was unbearable. You then had all the friends of friends and people in the street who would take it upon themselves to diagnose Ginge. Now considering he had a life limiting condition, it's not exactly rocket science to think that weight loss goes with Muscular Dystrophy is it? But no, these

Professor Winstons who had too much time on their hands, started a rumour that Ginge was anorexic. This was hurtful, unhelpful and total bollocks. A few times I would be out and someone would stop me, saying *"I've heard Damien is anorexic"* and I would then explain that it couldn't be further from the truth. They would go on and on trying to convince me, as they obviously thought I had my head in the sand until the point where I would just tell them to fuck off and walk away.

Yep you're right that it didn't probably help much, and I would have to listen to my mum or nan at some point once the person who had received the go forth advice had moaned. I just don't get human nature. I've seen it at its very best when it's helped me and my family when we have been on our knees, but I've seen some right fuck wits who have asked questions or passed comment when it's just not the right time.

One time was funny though. Ginge had been rough for a few weeks and suddenly had a good couple of weeks. I was off to Amsterdam to recharge my batteries for the weekend and two of my friends said if Dames fancied a night in the Dam they would come out with him for the day and night. The job of letting my mum know was given to me by Ginge and my pals. She wasn't impressed and made it clear she didn't want him to go, but would let us make the sensible decision, so obviously we went! He came out and was on top form holding court. I mean the boys literally listened to his every word. He was so sharp. He was ripping the piss out of me nonstop and I loved every second of it, as I had my Ginge's back. Anyway, we returned and he was good for a few weeks, but then he got a bit rough again and was poorly at home. I popped to the shops and this old girl stopped me and her grandson had come to Amsterdam with us. Well, she has obviously seen Dames recently looking skinny. She heard he had been to Amsterdam and she then goes *"I think he needs to get up to Kings and get himself checked out in case it's a dose."* I was literally in tears. I must have got back home faster than Nigel Mansell as I couldn't wait to tell him and take the piss. I was crying so much I had to tell my mum who went mad and was going to pull the lady when she saw her. Me and the boys wound him up for weeks.

I was always left with the shit jobs to do. He was in Lane Fox Unit once and one evening we were all meant to be going to see Blur at Brixton Academy. I was going to see him early afternoon as I was still going to the concert and I got a text saying can you collect my Vals (Valentino Jeans for those not about then) from the cleaners, get the old girl to iron me a shirt and bring me a decent jumper up. My mum was going *"Well at least he hasn't lost his pride"*. Hmmmm, I started to smell a rat. Once at the hospital I got the *"I don't ask you for much"* speech and that meant I had to convince nurses and doctors that it was ok to take a sick man to a concert. I somehow pulled this off but needed a break and thought I will tell my mum later. So off we went, about ten of us.

After the concert Dames was in no rush to get back to the hospital, even finding time to grab chicken and chips and he wandered back onto the ward around 1am. I went home to be confronted by my mum who had gone to visit him, only to be told "his brother" had taken him to a Blur concert. Ginge left me to take the bollocking of all bollockings, saying *"You know what Mum's like when someone upsets her"*. Would I do it again? Of course. I would pay a lot of money just for him to ask me to do anything.

In around 2000 we noticed a huge decline in Dames' health, but I can remember to the day that I knew he was in a bad way. It was a Saturday in February 2002 and Millwall were away to Nottingham Forest. I wasn't on great form myself as I had gone out on a bender straight from work on the Friday. I came out of the kebab drinking hole at gone 6.30am, went home, changed clothes and tried to freshen up, but it just wasn't working. Dames had been poorly all week but Millwall were playing well and there were about twenty of us all going so he pushed and came with us. We had a good laugh and Millwall won 2-1. It was a really blustery day and as we were walking across the Trent Bridge to the train station, I noticed Dames fighting for breath and was going blue. We got him in a pub (as most blokes do in an emergency), out of the wind and he felt a bit better, but as soon as he went to go out it happened again. One of the boys ran on to the station and got a taxi. One thing about my pals, and it was a Millwall thing as well, you all stick together. We got him to the station and as we tried to get on a train a guard said I couldn't sit with him. I tried in vain to explain but he wasn't having it as Millwall fans were jumping in giving their opinion. I looked at Ginge who said *"I will be fine, I just want to get home"*. A sensible copper said *"Look son, sit where you are meant to and if anything happens, I promise I will get you"*. On the train our pals were asking questions I just didn't have the answers to, and I was scared, so scared. Most of all, from a selfish point of view, I was gutted. The bloke I idolised was fucked and both me and Ginge knew it. That was the start of my heart breaking.

From then on it was a never ending story of hospital stays and negative news. My mum was in pieces as I acted like the family cheerleader always looking for that bit of positive information to grab. *"Mum, I'm in the pub with Ginge and he is eating a ham roll"*. This snippet would lift the whole family as Dames was now under 5st. I would regularly walk to McDonald's in the cold and rain to get him a chicken nugget Happy Meal, as a full plate of food made him feel sick. A kid's meal was a result if he ate half.

All that way for four nuggets knowing he would only eat two, but those two would be like nuggets of gold. My mum was the same. He would eat a Penguin bar, boom, my mum was off, down the Walworth Road buying up packs of them, only for Ginge not to eat another for three weeks!

My mum would often be in tears and I felt so useless. Watching the two people closest to you fall apart was horrendous and I was in denial. I was the man of the house, the big brother who thought a Lorenzo's Oil type story was unfolding and I was waiting for that doctor to land at Heathrow Airport with a cure for my brother. What a mug I was, but it kept me sane and It's writing this that I start to remember what a bastard of an illness Muscular Dystrophy is and how being in denial is a much happier place.

I was there 24/7 for Ginge. Then every Friday I would sit with him until about 10pm and he would say *"Why don't you go out?"* I would say *"Nah, I'll stay with you"*. Then he would go *"There might even be an ugly fat bird for you to get your nuts in with"*. See even in dark times brothers can't help sticking the boot in.

Then at 10.30pm I was out the door on the agreement that if he felt ill, he would get my mum to text me. I would walk into a pub or bar only for everyone to want to know about Ginge, but I just wanted to tell them to piss off. They all had the best intentions and good wishes but none were going to help Ginge. I knew I had about seven hours in me and I just wanted that Jack Daniels and as many as possible to take this pain away. I wanted to get so smashed that when I woke up I wouldn't know where I was for the first thirty seconds and not worry about Ginge. This was my time.

But there were so many funny stories during what was an incredibly sad time. We bonded as a trio as no family I know ever have. Our life was Ginge's room, the kitchen and his health. Dinners were cooked with bottles of wine on the go and stories were told as we all got to know each other as individuals, more than most siblings and parents ever do.

I remember one New Year's Eve all my pals wanted to go to Greenwich and I just didn't want to be away From Dames, so I swerved it. We ordered an Indian around 8pm, I had a bottle of JD on the go and my mum was steaming into a box of wine. Dames was in bed while I sat in his room and put a boring documentary box set on; I think it was the latest Michael Palin which had about six episodes. Me and Ginge sat up watching it and then called my mum in for midnight. All the crisps and nuts were out. She then went back to her puzzle in the kitchen listening to our every word and she was loving every one of them. At 4am we went to bed united as a family and with priceless memories nothing could buy and no one could take away. To make it even better I bumped into my pals about 10am on New Year's Day as I was on the bookies run for my brother. They had a crap night and had paid about £250 each for the privilege.

One Friday night Dames burst into life, got up and organised a pizza. I was going to Bruges the next day to visit my pals and had debated on having some blonde highlights. I asked my mum to get the dye and Ginge suggested she did it now. Stupidly I agreed and let a pissed-up mother ruin my hair. This resulted in me getting absolutely ruined by my pals on our weekend away and this was orchestrated by Ginge who had even texted them before I left the house.

Ginge was never one to show great emotion. I'm much more emotional than him, but I keep my guard up and I don't talk to anyone about my condition. What's the point? All the talking in the world isn't going to change it, is it? Even with Kellie there are still things I don't openly tell her; it's just she has got better at spotting the signs and has her own tactics to get them out of me. Ginge was a closed book and he wasn't giving anything away, certainly not to those he saw on a daily basis. I think a girl called Laura from Liverpool who he really did love might have got some of his inner feelings out of him.

Once, just once, did he show some emotion and it was one of the most humbling feelings I've ever felt. We had gone to the Oval for our annual trip to the Test Match with the chaps. Ginge, with hindsight, just wasn't up to it as it was a cold blustery day and nothing like the August day it should have been. He hung around long enough to see his demi God Andrew Flintoff get a half century and after lunch I suggested he should head home and rest. Now our house was only a fifteen minute walk from

192

the Oval, but I could tell he was dreading it. I said I would get one of the boys to take him home but he wouldn't have wanted them to miss the cricket so I went to the main gates and hailed a black cab down. I told the driver to wait (meter running of course) then drop my brother off and bring my pal back. I got Dames round to the cab quickly and texted my mum who worked in the school across the road telling her to have the house ready. My pal was back at the match within twenty minutes, so for Dames it was less than ten. Then an hour later I got the most heartfelt text thanking me for helping him and saying he had the best brother in the world. I bluffed and said *"Oh you'd do the same for me"* and I made it sound like it was just a favour, but after I wiped a tear away, I felt so proud.

In the early hours of Tuesday 08.03.05. my life changed for the worse, forever, and I would never get over this. It wasn't how I thought it would happen as it was so calm. With a tear running down her cheek my mum walked in calmly, so calmly that I thought she was coming to tell me some unimportant news, but the tears gave me a pre warning. It was 3am and before my brain could digest everything, she went *"He's gone"*.

I knew who and what she meant and just said *"Get Big Marc"*. Big Marc has been one of my closest friends all my life and we've gone through primary, junior and secondary school together. He is a big strapping black lad who is one of the kindest and gentlest people you could wish to know. He was always different to my other friends which is nothing to do with skin colour, as to me Marc is Marc but he was different because he had a brain and wasn't into the same silliness as the rest of us. He was a safe pair of hands and the nearest I have ever had to a big brother. Big

Marc arrived within minutes. He grew up two doors away from us but was dating my aunt who later became his wife and her house was only a few minutes away. As soon as he walked in I could see he was in tears himself. I had to get up and got it into my head I could save Ginge. I was like a man obsessed. *"Let me get up!"* I was screaming at my mum, Marc and my Uncle Malc, who had now arrived. In the end my uncle said just help him up and I was up in minutes. Me and Ginge had a saying, *"Never stop believing"* and we had nicked it from Only Fools and Horses. Just let me in there, I will say a few words and get him going. Even sitting next to him holding his cold hand and talking, I still couldn't take it in that he had gone.

The door burst open and my dad rushed in, screaming at everyone, calling them all sorts of names. It was probably shock or anger, but most of all it was not on. No one had been anything but supportive to Ginge and as quickly as my dad had arrived, he had gone again. I just sat there with Ginge until the moment I realised he had actually gone. Then I just got up, went into my room and closed the doors. I asked to be left alone and I sat there for around four hours. Then I heard my mum's voice. Like a switch being turned on in my head I then thought of nothing but my mum and what she must have been going through. My job now was to support her through this and look after her, which helped me immensely as it didn't give me time to grieve, but long term it wouldn't do me any good as I needed to get some of this grief out of my system.

It was straight into organising a funeral. The only thing I knew Dames wanted was to go to Albin's and Sons in Bermondsey. These people were the real deal and people often say you get

194

what you pay for in life. Well, Albin's were so classy and the respect they showed myself and my mum took so much pressure off us. They were brilliant people. I'll tell you something, the only time I cried through all of this was at the meeting at Albin's. The Funeral Director asked if there were any places he would like to pass on his final journey and as I started to say the word Millwall I just broke down.

I never cried over Ginge until about five years later when I was married, and Kellie managed to get all the emotion out of me. I'm not one for pouring my heart out, and I didn't want to ruin a good day for my mum and start going on about Ginge. With Kellie it was different as if you can't be honest to your Mrs who is also your best friend, who can you be honest with?

The funeral was packed. I think over two hundred people came to the service and so many more lined John Ruskin Street. To see so much love and respect for your brother when you are so low is so humbling. The boys, our mates, had agreed to carry his coffin in and, wow, it was amazing just watching a group of blokes who had never taken much seriously in life just go into action. Dames dying messed them up too. We've all had falling outs since and some we have sorted out, some we haven't, but I will always owe a debt to them for the love and support they gave me and my mum. The service went quickly and I'm not sure if that is a good thing or not, as, although you are desperate to get out of there you need a passage on this final journey and a service is part of it. Father David had done his research on Ginge. Like the time the Italian tourists thought he was a beggar up Oxford Street. He was dolled right up and had put his baseball cap on his tray. They put some change in it and walked off, but

Ginge being a diamond gave it to the first homeless person he saw. He also told the story of Dames' obsession with competitions. He would go in for any, and one time he won a set of roller skates. The company telephoned him with the good news; all you could hear was *"Mate I'm in a poxy wheelchair what the f**k do I want with a set of roller skates?"* Me and my mum were in tears of laughter in the kitchen at the time listening to the conversation, but Father David being the top man he is, managed to combine the humour and sadness that the event needed. He broke it up with some music playing *'Don't look Back in Anger'* by Oasis, a song my brother always loved. He then played *'Hey Jude'* by The Beatles which was my brother's favourite song and little did I know then what a part the name Jude would play in my life years later. The final song could only be *'Let 'em Come'*. A song that meant so much to so many there.

I couldn't get away fast enough. I needed a drink and at that stage I don't think I understood what a big part drink played in my life. I was first back to the Beehive pub, a place Ginge loved. I drank from around 4pm until 5am the next morning, people were buying me drinks and at that stage it seemed great just to make me numb, but I just needed to sit down and cry my eyes out and I didn't know how to. I was scared that if I did cry I would never stop and I couldn't cry. I needed to be strong for my mum.

The next few months were a nightmare. I had returned to work only to walk out numerous times. I had so much anger in me. I would have a junkie sitting in front of me telling me how shit life was and how they wanted to be dead. Well, a good bloke did die and he didn't want to die but he did. These people were making

196

me sick. I was also drinking so much and I had a plan; drink wine with my mum on a weekday and then go out and get smashed on the weekend. But trouble was coming my way as I was getting into stupid situations.

One Tuesday I bunked work and at 2pm went to a bar called Monaghan's on the Walworth Road. I had no rush to get home as my mum was in Greece and I wanted to be on my own. I drank drink after drink then at about 8pm I went for a walk to another pub. As I've gone to cross by the McDonald's, some bloke in a car flew round and just missed me. Regardless of who's fault it was, he was going too fast, but he slammed the brakes on and got out. We are now in the middle of a slanging match and as we are standing outside Walworth Police Station it didn't take long for two coppers to come over. They sent the bloke off which really wound me up and now it's me arguing with the coppers. They took me into the police station and by now I'm anti-social Fred as I feel aggrieved. I'm telling them they should be out doing real police work, but they were actually nice blokes and just wanted me to sober up and get home. They found my mobile but it had a lock on it and wouldn't open and asked why I was so drunk. I then poured my heart out and I actually felt better. I sobered up quickly, apologised and asked if I could go home. They said I could but they would have to take me and as I couldn't get into a police car, we would have to walk. Shit, if anyone my mum knows finds out they will tell her within minutes and she will kill me. We took a long walk home going through as many back streets as possible.

A few months later the booze got me in trouble again. I had been out and was smashed. My cousin Pikey was out with us and he had had enough by about 3am so went home for a lay down but said he would let me in. About 5am I walked home on my own as I needed to get some fresh air. I have always had trouble supporting myself in the chair so I have a chest belt and like most blokes who have had a skin full I think I'm stronger than I am and can't be told anything. I'm walking down my street in the road as the pavements are awful and dangerous and as I went over a sleeping policeman too fast, I flew forward. Now only the tray is stopping me from falling on the floor and on top of that I was in the middle of John Ruskin Street which is busy at any time. I was stopping all the traffic passing, but I just didn't have the strength to lift myself up. After a few minutes the cars are about six or seven backed up and a few drivers come over to me mostly to shout "get out of the fucking road". A couple of drivers tried a half-hearted attempt to ask what was wrong and with slurred speech and the position I was in they must have thought I was special needs. Then one flags down a police van and I'm like *"Don't mate, please, this is all too much"*. The police came over and rather dramatically start shining a torch in my face and asking me if I'm ok. I kept telling them to push me back from my chest but they weren't listening though. Finally, I get one who listens, he pushed me back and, in a split second, I'm upright and ready to go. I said my apologies to the drivers who have been delayed and with a *"Thanks lads"* I attempted to have it through the slips. Unfortunately, the copper in charge started going all Juliet Bravo on me and said he had a duty of care to get me home to a responsible adult. Fuck me, I'm in it now, the Old Girl will kill me. I laid my cards on the table and said *"Look mate I can't have your van outside my house"*. I explained why and they asked who else I can get. Eureka! My cousin Pikey is at home and I telephoned seven or eight times but the div didn't answer. Blimey Pikey, for the first time in your life you could be classed as a responsible adult. Me and two of the Met's finest started taking a slow walk down and as we got within twenty metres out comes Pikey in his shorts. I beckoned him towards us and they seemed to want to talk for ages, but finally they left.

Did I learn my lesson? Nope. About a month later I did the same and fell forward in the garden. It was a bitter night and honestly I would have died there if some young bird hadn't heard me calling out and came in. I was so lucky with that one. I think I was just going through a time in my life when I was so reckless. I would do anything just to get away from the memory of Ginge.

Nowadays I struggle in a different way. Since Jude's come into my life, I get upset that Dames didn't get the chance to be a dad. I appreciate everything I have and so much more, but sometimes I'm in tears to Kellie.

He was the real deal, the main man.

When someone dies you get so many stories, but with Dames he was just unique. I always say I won the lottery of life getting him as my brother and I'm blessed with some amazing memories that other people would love to have with their siblings. I miss him like crazy. What I would do to put Jude into his arms for five minutes or for him to have a pizza with Kellie so they can discuss me being hard work. He was the best brother anyone could want. Funny, clever, so ahead of his time and he knew all the clothes or music before we did, but most of all he was fiercely loyal. He was so intelligent and he could have done anything he wanted, but all he wanted was to be a good bloke and that he truly was. A part of me died with Ginge but luckily I had two saviours in Kellie and Jude and they've given me the determination to push on. He would want me to give them my all.

Wherever you are Ginge, there isn't a day you are not mentioned in our house. You still rule the roost and I owe you so much. You gave me the blue print on how to deal with this shit illness.

Love you loads mate. Xx

IT AIN'T OVER 'TIL IT'S OVER

Annus horribilus, Your Majesty? I've had one of those... But I must still be a little positive as I survived what was the shittiest year ever. 2013 was just a fucker.

From the very start it was poxy. My uncle Malcolm, who I was so, so close to, was diagnosed with cancer and it knocked us all for six. Malc was your prime example of a Marmite person and people seemed to love him or hate him, but for me he was someone I just found infectious; I loved listening to the stories. I loved the fact that he wanted the best for me. So, when his condition deteriorated as fast as it did, it just did not seem real. I was constantly in contact with him by text or emails and he lived in Gloucester, so it was a schlep to see him, in fact impossible with my health being so poor.

The texts continued until one day I didn't get one. That day my mum told me that he was extremely ill, and texting wasn't an option for him anymore. His wife Margaret and kids Dan, Flora and Fran were so grown up despite being teenagers. They showed so much class and dignity throughout and when the sad day came that he passed away in early February, life seemed so shitty, but it was about to get even worse. My mum had been ill for months and we will have a chat about all that later. She had cancer of the womb a few years earlier, underwent a hysterectomy and beat it. All during Malc's illness she was complaining of being sick, tired, run down and had a recurring chest infection. Not surprising I thought, as she was so close to her big brother, and a week after Malc's funeral she was still feeling really rough. By now she had gone through about three or four courses of antibiotics. I remember her struggling to get down the stairs one day and when she finally did, I said "I'm taking you to the hospital". She was adamant she wouldn't go, but I just told Kellie to get the car ready and twenty minutes later we were at Guy's Hospital. That's when I knew she was ill as Mum didn't put up the usual arguments or just say she wasn't going.

Kellie had to park the car so I went ahead with my mum. She was literally holding onto my shoulder to stay up. I was driving an electric wheelchair badly while trying to keep her upright and fighting back the tears. I just knew she was ill. You just know these things about people close to you.

In Minor Injuries they carried out an x ray and said she was recovering from a chest infection; we presumed the same one she had tried to shift for months. The doctor gave her a form for a blood test, and she was sent on her way, but she just wanted to get home. By chance I had a district nurse visiting me the next day and when he saw my mum, how pale and weak she looked, he offered to do the blood test and send it off the same day. We encouraged her to rest up and hoped that she would turn the corner. The next day we received a rather strange telephone call from our GP, Dr Sinha. He is rather eccentric but a lovely bloke and has looked after us all our lives. He just said that my mum had to go to the hospital immediately for a repeat blood test. We later found out that he knew the diagnosis and he could just not bring himself to tell her or us.

Kellie took my mum straight back to Guy's Hospital with her good friend, Edna. She then headed back to the house to await news. I am not too sure what I was expecting. It was about 3pm on a cold Thursday afternoon in February and I just presumed it would be a case of more antibiotics or an overnight stay. But looking back even then I still questioned at the time my normal stay calm attitude. At around 6pm Kellie went to collect Edna as they were keeping my mum in hospital. Common sense told me they were doing more tests or keeping her in to get to the bottom of it all. Kellie had already taken Edna home, opened our front door, walked in calmly and sat down, which was a major success for someone who is a softy and cries at anything. As I asked how Mum was getting on, Kellie just said *"She's got Leukaemia"*. For about fifteen seconds I just carried on talking. I'm a bit mutton and just presumed I had misheard her. Then boom, I heard her say it again and it was like a metal bar over the top of my head. I felt sick and cold. I couldn't get the words out to ask questions but in reality, what questions were there to be asked? This is about as serious as it can get.

As per usual Kellie was the most amazing person you could wish and need for. She cuddled me and cuddled me and just said calm down. Her own tears dripped on my neck. They felt like ice, everything seemed so cold in the world at this point, I felt warm being embraced by her and for ten minutes couldn't face moving. Not even to find out about my mum. I was weak, scared and lost. Being in Kellie's arms felt like safety.

After what seemed like the longest and scariest ten minutes ever, it was time to get my shit together. My mum needed me. We are tough, I kept telling myself, but this was going to be our

Armageddon. This had come from nowhere and we always knew we would have a few dire moments due to Muscular Dystrophy, but this was a curve ball and it had taken us all out. "Get up man!", I kept telling myself, and it worked. Finally, I got my head in place to ask Kellie what was happening and basically, there was no real news. The second blood test had confirmed Leukaemia and she had been moved to a specialist ward and would see a consultant in the morning.

"Telephone Uncle Billy" I said to Kellie. I've told you about my Uncle, he actually believes he knows everything about any subject. If he doesn't, he will give himself enough time to find an answer. He actually thinks he knows a bit about medicine too and the thing is I love him to death. He is my main man, my go to person and he can wind me up like only my brother and Mrs can. He seems to take everyone's side but mine. If I tell him something then I'm wrong. Honestly if it was World War II and my house had been bombed by Germans I could say *"fucking Luftwaffe"* and he would say *"It's your own fault for not checking your black out* curtains". However, he has my back and wants the best for me. His constant questioning of what I do and why I do it is priceless. It keeps my feet on the ground, and I think many kids miss that male role model today. I pray Jude has an Uncle Billy to push him on and ask the awkward questions. Uncle Billy isn't a bullshitter and he isn't going to give you false hope. I mean this is the man who regularly speaks to people about planning their own funeral, pukka chat that in the pub on a Saturday.

So, when he said *"Oh fuck"* when Kellie told him the news it didn't overly scare me. He said his usual wise words and it has always given me some comfort over the years. *"Get all the information you can from the doctors, stay calm and let them do their job".*

After the chat with Uncle Billy it was time to text my mum.

What do you say to someone in that situation? I just put *"Alright Mum"* and a kiss. Straight away she was asking if I was ok, she was always thinking of others. We exchanged pleasantries for a bit, then it was a case of her saying that she wasn't expecting all this crap. We said goodnight after a short flurry of text messages with me being told to be at the hospital at 10am, as she would be meeting her consultant then. As she reminded me, we will do this like we've done everything else, as a family.

The next morning we met the consultant who told us details of a combination of chemotherapy they would be starting and that these days the prognosis for AML (Acute Myeloid Leukaemia) was good; the treatment would start that day. With all the problems we had going on around us, if life wasn't difficult enough at that time already, I then became sick myself.

I had been complaining of a cold and I was told by my mum's doctors not to visit her due to her low immunity from the chemotherapy. I actually got the cold that we would later discover was combined Swine and Bird Flu (H1N3), during a visit to my mum while she was in Guy's. Some dirty fucker sneezed on me while we were in some carousel doors near the main entrance. People ask me how I knew it was him. I just do, I can remember it like it was yesterday.

Over the next few days my breathing got worse and my throat felt like it was closing. I didn't want to go to hospital, I had enough going on, but by the third night of not sleeping (I hadn't slept properly for weeks), Kellie called an ambulance. It was Wednesday 20th March, around three to four weeks after my mum was admitted. The usual hospital process of going to A&E and then round to the Lane Fox Unit took a massive change of direction when they said, *"We need to get him up to Intensive Care".*

I remember feeling drained and also like shit. I would describe it as feeling like I had been on a three-day bender and had just woken up, only to have to step into the ring with Tyson Fury to do twelve rounds. I just wanted to sleep. I mean I hadn't slept properly for days, even weeks. On top of all that they had just stuck a catheter in so I was in a fair bit of pain. I was drifting into a deep sleep and Kellie had mentioned my kidneys were playing up. Every time I came around, I seemed to have someone doing something with a face mask on and it scared me, but at that point I just wanted to sleep.

On the journey to ICU I woke up a bit. It was around 5am and I was freezing. I was whisked into an isolation room, again with every fucker wearing a mask. It was like rush hour in Tokyo Central and to think that these days with Covid-19 reaching our shores no one would take a second glance in today's world, but back then it was scary stuff. They told Kellie she had to wait in a relative's room while they made me comfortable. She argued and I argued but they weren't having any of it. ICU was a quite different place to the Lane Fox Unit and this was a different level.

Now, this next bit. The stuff I'm about to tell you, well it fucked me over and still does to this day. I'm far from dramatic and I'm pretty good at blocking out a lot of crap stuff, but not this.

I'm actually sitting here with a tear now……….

So, when Kellie left the room I had swine flu, bird flu and kidney damage and I was in a bad way. When she came back in, around twenty minutes later, I had been intubated and was on a ventilator, sedated and fighting for my life. To this day I don't know exactly what happened to go from being awake and very ill to the way I had deteriorated at this point in such a small space of time. I either had some form of seizure or an attack and I honestly don't want to know. It was never really discussed, and they just used the term *"a turn"*. I've never tried to get to the bottom of it and Kellie has always been intrigued, but, at my request, has not pushed it.

Trying to describe what happened and the experience of *"the turn"* is just so dramatic. I died that night; I know I did. My breathing was poor and all I remember is the doctors and nurses running around. There seemed to be hundreds, but more likely ten or twelve, but it seemed so chaotic, manic. I remember seeing and hearing people enticing me to stop, then some good people, my Uncle Shugs being one and was a figure I could see, but obviously wasn't there, telling me I had to do what I felt was right.

My Mum and Ginge were certainly there. I can see Ginge going to me *"It's not as bad as you think here mate, but you've got Mum and Kellie to look after, it's not your time yet"*. I wrestled between giving up and fighting, I could feel myself just wanting

207

to rest but I had these people screaming at me. *"Keep fighting Lee, don't give up"*.

Make of it what you want. I'm not here to convince you, I know what happened that night. Then I saw Kellie, well, an image of her, crying, and kept thinking we haven't made enough memories yet. That must have been when I kicked in and fought.

My pals are going to ruin me about this and I'm going to get all the David Icke jokes now. Only Kellie knows this happened to me and I honestly couldn't talk about it until now. I am in tears writing this as it still scares me today. I am not a drama queen and I have never mentioned it, but I think I have Post Traumatic Stress Disorder from it all. No good has really come from airing it. I am a proud man who is in denial that I suffer from anxiety and not sure why I haven't admitted it until now. The charlatans and attention seekers who have taken anxiety as *'their struggle'* have made me give it a big swerve. So, there you go. Behind all the tough guy charade is a bloke who sits up scared at night a few times a week and just doesn't want to speak about it.

This all happened early on the Thursday morning and Kellie must have been so scared. She had to have 'a chat' with a nurse in charge to inform her about my dramatic situation and after that she endured four days of me sedated, not knowing if I would come around or not. It was then three weeks of worry about whether I would get better, then finally three months of pushing me on and telling me I can do this. Don't forget she was balancing all of this with daily trips to see my mum who was battling Leukaemia and worrying about her son she couldn't visit. I guess you've already twigged that I think Kellie is the best thing since sliced bread. When people say *"She's a keeper"* they are forgetting she's Lev Yashin, Gordon Banks and Kasey Keller all rolled in to one. She is the kindest and most loyal person I've had the fortune to meet. I love her so much that it hurts.

After a few days in ICU they wanted to wake me up and it was a weird sensation. I came around with a right groggy head, Kellie cried and kissed me but I was in and out of it and kept falling back to sleep. A good friend Joanne came in, and I knew I was fucked because everyone had been crying, I noticed that straight away. They all had red eyes like they had been in a coffee shop just off Dam Square for the afternoon. It was while trying to talk to Joanne that I twigged my throat was sore and no words were coming out and I then clocked the number of machines I was rigged up to. *"Jesus, I'm fucked here"* I thought. I managed to mouth to Jo *"Am I going to be alright?"* and she just cuddled me and said *"Yes"*. For a split second I felt a little better and she explained I had Swine Flu. Kellie then came back to take control as Jo had obviously had to take a few seconds out after first seeing me. We just sat and held hands and between the maze of wires she somehow managed to get her head on my chest. She said *"I love you"* and I mouthed *"I love you more"* which was our little thing between us and it still is. From then I knew I could find a way out of this and I nodded off back to sleep.

The next few days were spent with doctors deciding what to do with me. A popular chappy like myself had loads of visitors even though it was meant to be immediate family only, and quite a few strings (string vest = pest) made an appearance, but they all meant well. I was grateful to everyone who cares about me but I was scared and felt like shit. One good thing about coming out of sedation was the nurses would say he may drop back off to sleep. Quite a few times I did, just to escape the silence as no one really knew what to say to me.

The relief of waking up and seeing Kellie quickly evaporated with concerns around my health and how I was going to get myself out of there. I always back myself; I always have done. I know my limitations, but also know what I can achieve. I'm not a doctor and distance myself from all medical stuff about me. Why the fuck after a day of coming around and still being in danger, did I start to worry about getting better and up and about? I was told just to rest and I still felt like shit. The flu was attacking me still on all fronts but I tried to rest although I felt sick all the time. I had so many drugs being pumped into me that I was constantly as high as a kite which was quite a good feeling at first, but soon went, as the sickness was making me feel so ill.

After a few days I noticed they were trying to come up with a plan of action for me but it had already been stated that I would be on a ventilator for life. Fuck that, I'm thinking, but if I'm being honest with myself, I just couldn't take anything on. They started talking about tracheostomies and I had seen people with them when I was in the Lane Fox Unit but being a total big tart they had always made me feel sick to look at. I'm a wimp and on top of that I've always hated people touching my Adam's apple to, the extent where I wouldn't even let Kellie kiss around the front of my neck while she was trying her daily attempts to seduce me. Dr Davidson, my Consultant before I got sick, wanted me to have a trach for a while due to my body getting weaker over time, but I always swerved the conversation. It would be put on the let's talk about it next time I have an appointment agenda.

Looking back, having a trach put in was always going to be in a do or die situation. Now all bets were off, I needed the trach.

Kellie tried to tell me I didn't have any chance of getting out of their ICU let alone the hospital without a trach. Like most blokes, I don't listen to my wife when it matters, and I summoned the doctor in charge to try and take control of the situation. I wanted my cuirass which was the old machine I had been using to help my breathing at night. I needed comfort. They were mortified. To put it into perspective, it would be like insisting on the crappy old Daisy Wheel printers you had in the 80's and shunning a brand-new Laser Ink Jet printer. To imagine the cuirass, think of an old Iron Lung, but just around my chest pushing up and down. It was an old relic of medical equipment, but I had fallen in love with it. The sensation it gave me once I got onto my bed and it started working and I suddenly found I was breathing about 20% better than I had before. The medical people were fascinated by how it still kept me alive and had no interest in ever letting me use it again.

Once the doctor came in I tried to explain that I wanted the cuirass on but communication was hard as I had this massive tube in my mouth. Finally, I got my point across to which she just said *"no"*. There was no discussion just a 100% negative response, but being a stubborn person, I asked every day and I asked the consultant in charge. In the end they must have got bored of me and said they would let me let try it at my own risk. If I could slap my hands together loudly and rub them like Del Trotter, this would be the moment to do it as I was so confident it would work. They fired up the cuirass. I'm not sure if the amassed medical audience was there as a precaution, infringement or waiting to pounce to section me. The cuirass came on and they switched the ventilator off. Like an asteroid crashing towards earth my oxygen level went from 98% to 85% in a minute. It was dropping even more but I couldn't focus on the equipment as I was struggling to breathe. The sweat was pouring off me. I felt lightheaded and knew I had made a mistake. I shouted with no sound *"get me back on the fucking ventilator"* and after a few minutes I started to feel a bit better. Then the realisation that I was going to be on a ventilator for life hit home and I waited for Kellie to leave the room before I cried my eyes out.

So, a trachi it is then! My nurse Kelly Stewart came up from the Lane Fox Unit and I look at her like the little sister I've never had. She is someone who cares so much and can be a softy when needed, but put you in line when you are playing up. I had ignored a lot of the trachi talk so Kelly talked me through it and made me see sense. The penny had finally dropped and if I didn't have the trachi then I wasn't leaving ICU. I'll be on a ventilator for life. How will I cope with that? Do I have the ability to do this? Was my life about to change dramatically? Will I still be Lee? But in all honesty, it was all irrelevant for now, I needed to get out and support my mum and the Mrs, the wife who had held our family together. All the questions could wait and it was time to take a step forward. Kellie made it clear to me that the trachi was my only real option. She was amazing as she calmed my fears, but never deviated from what she knew I needed. That's the priceless gift of having a wife who is also your soul mate. They have that ability to be able to say what a wife or partner needs to say, but as a friend knows when to say it. A couple of days before I had one of those eureka moments, I thought that if I put my hand at the correct angle I'll be able to write. Once I cracked it, I was buzzing. I grabbed some paper and as I wrote I could see the worry in Kellie's eye. I'm sure she would have been thinking that it was going to be a negative and probably quite brutal reply. It wasn't. I simply wrote *"Trachi for the good-looking bloke in the corner".* Her eyes sparkled and she smiled. So did I, and even though I was approaching my worst nightmare, her smile still lifted me.

I was now asking if I could have it done that day, talk about going from one extreme to the other. Unfortunately, there was a bit of a wait and it took around eight days before they even got around to doing it and that was torture. I was getting impatient because I needed to get out of there. Trying to talk was a nightmare but using pen and paper was a breakthrough and the only problem was when I would write a message using the C or F word, Kellie being nice would edit it from my quote as she read it out, which drove me mad. The days dragged and the nights were even longer, and people started to fall into set routines when visiting. My dad is about as much good as a chocolate lifeguard in these situations. He just can't cope with anything. He finds himself a role and then makes that his job everyday so he can get out of the hospital. I was on nil by mouth the whole time I was in ICU and all I had was those foam swabs to rub in my mouth. I would bite into the swabs to get that last drop of water out, but somehow I talked the doctors into letting me have five millilitres of sarsaparilla a day through a syringe. I must have been a total string to them as they often relented to shut me up. They agreed that once a day I could dip three syringes in a drink.

I said Orange Fanta so my dad would go off for a walk to get one from McDonald's, thus walking past numerous shops that sold cans of Fanta. He would be gone for hours as he just needed to get out of the hospital. Why, I understand, but it was a luxury I didn't have.

My Uncle Billy would come in and he has a strange thought process. He always wants to get you angry it seems. He would come and constantly tell me to sort myself out and as he went to go home, he would say *"Right I'm off for a kebab and a beer. If you weren't in here you could have one too"*. It drove me mad and I wanted to get up and ram that doner kebab down his throat. It worked through and he got me through it. Don't get me wrong, it drove me mad, but I got angry and I needed that.

Getting out for refreshments wasn't the only incentive to get back to good health urgently. I hadn't seen my mum and this concerned me. When I spoke about her everyone would tell me she was doing well but without much detail, so it was clear to me she was still in a bad way. I needed to see her with my own eyes as this was tearing me apart; I was failing as her son at this time. I had to focus on getting out, setting some goals, even if they were very small basic ones. I got a nurse and Kellie to get some paper and I started compiling a list of drinks I would drink once I was out. I would then spend hours putting numbers next to them in preference. Was it torture? Oh yes, but again, it worked.

The nights were horrible as you just can't sleep. I got scared quite a lot and my mates will take the piss, but I did. I think it all hit home when I was on my Pat (Pat Malone = on your own). One night I got scared about 11pm and I thought I ain't getting out of here. I need to see Kellie one more time. I made the hospital telephone her and send her up. I felt bad but I needed her to see I was convinced I wasn't getting out.

Finally, the day came for the trachi to go in. I wasn't really that scared and if someone had told me three months before I was having a tube drilled in to my throat I would have winced and nearly passed out, but by now I wanted it done. I needed to take a step forward after a month or so of being dragged down. When the time came the anaesthetist put the needle in, pushed the knockout juice in and asked me to count backwards from one hundred. As I got into the eighties and the looks between the surgeon, doctors and nurses became apparent, I thought here we go. I was still wide awake. They started having a quick tête-à-tête and then the anaesthetist said *"Mr Evans are you a big boy?"* I thought that's a bit previous and I've never had any complaints. Not much praise but no complaints. I told him I was about thirteen stone and he seemed a little shocked, even more shocked when I told him I was six foot one. He pulled the blanket back to have a look at me and smiled, they had been working out the amount of anaesthetic for someone a lot smaller. Once they worked out the correct dose, I got to ninety-seven I think, and I was gone, lights out.

I awoke a few hours later and didn't feel too bad, but looking out of the corner of my eye I was aware of a tube going side on into my throat. There was no real pain, but I could feel something there. I was amazed that the large tube that had been sitting in my mouth for nearly a month was now gone. It made it a little easier to try and speak or mouth words, but there was still no sound. I looked up and clocked a stunning young blonde nurse and asked *"Nurse, are you married?"* I was conscious of someone else in the room and as I turned my head my Mrs was giving me the *'I don't know about her but you are'* look. It was the drugs; they mess with your mind.

I was just glad to have taken a step forward. I'm a positive person but the last few months had taken its toll and if I'm honest not much had changed as I was still in ICU, but I felt I had made that first step. The next few days the euphoria rubbed off, but not quickly as I was still thinking positively. I'm impatient and I want to test myself and put down markers. When they said a speech therapist would come the next day to check I was swallowing properly and not restricting my throat, I was awake at 8am waiting for her. When she didn't come by 6pm I was gutted. It was actually nine days before I saw her and in that period I was a total pain in the arse to Kellie and the nurses. I just wanted to take control of this and I didn't care about the speech therapist. I was being told I might not be able to eat or drink again and honestly, without showing off, I thought now bollocks to that. I had a nice rib eye or jalfrezi on my mind with a cold Becks and can of Coke. After going through all of this, not eating or drinking just wasn't an option for me.

While in ICU I couldn't see my mum as she was in Guy's Hospital having chemotherapy and she finally got out the day before her birthday. The doctors told her to go home and rest, but being her, she told the consultant she was coming to see me on her birthday and by now they knew what she was like. The dangers of having Leukaemia and visiting a hospital ward with no immunity and its germs wasn't going to stop her from visiting me and to top it off she wanted to surprise me.

I woke up early on her birthday and I was so glad she would be home. I knew many people would visit her and make a fuss of her and as disappointed as I was not to be part of it, I was smiling. At about 10am I looked up to see Kellie coming in. As I looked again, I could see my mum walking in. It was the most unreal feeling. As she got closer we both just cried. She cuddled me up and we sat there not speaking, just crying and hugging for a few minutes. Once we composed ourselves and stopped, we noticed that Kellie and my mum's friend, Edna, were still in tears. We then had two nurses tell us it was the most emotional and brilliant thing that they had seen.

After the hugging, tears and elation, it was back to normal life for a few minutes with some gallows humour. My mum had pushed her health to the limit in visiting me that day. I looked at her and seeing the hair loss through her chemotherapy was like a solid hard punch in the stomach. She had kept a little bit at the top like a tuft of hair. Out of nowhere I went *"Mum you really look like Jimmy Somerville now"*. Oh, we laughed and laughed. All through life silliness has kept me sane and it did that day.

We needed that day to lift us all.

Even in shit situations something amazing can come, that's the way it goes, but to quote Clarence Worley in True Romance *"But don't forget, it goes the other way too"*. That day it did.

I finally got to see the speech therapist and had my long-awaited move to the Lane Fox Unit. The speech therapist was telling me to eat yogurts for at least a week. Fuck that. Honestly, sometimes you have to just go for it and I nodded politely as she gave me four yogurts and said *"hopefully in two weeks you can try a soft bit of chocolate".* Leave off love, I've got bigger fish to fry, and with that, Kellie was sent to McDonald's to get me a burger, nuggets and fries. One of the doctors looked in and laughed and as I was eating, I'm thinking this is the first decent grub I've had in five weeks. I was Hank (Hank Marvin = starving), I didn't even feel the trachi and it was great to have some real food inside me. The speech therapist told me after that she had never seen anyone with a new trachi, eat solid food like that so soon before.

But nothing goes to plan for me, not whinging, but something will mess up. After a few days I got a severe stomach infection. My temperature went through the roof and there was some talk of sending me back to ICU. I was in a right pickle, but I couldn't have that as I needed to move forward, not go back.

It was a long weekend and it coincided with Millwall being at Wembley in the FA Cup semi-final. I never believed I would miss a big Millwall game but as gutted as I was, I was so rough I was sleeping through the coverage. I needed a central line put in my artery and a doctor was called out. He came in looking like a biker. Big ginger fuzzy beard and ripped Jeans and I'm thinking this bloke can't be the doctor. He was and he was superb. He said I'll have to put it in your neck and the nurse started telling me I needed to shave. I had a bit of a beard developing but wasn't in the mood to get the shaver out and start grooming myself. The nurse wouldn't let it go and boom, the doctor pipes up to her *"Look its fine. He's said no. If he said no on religious grounds you would let it go, so let it go here".* While he was setting up, he was telling me he was a doctor for years on oil rigs in the North Sea and has seen everything. He knew his stuff and got me sorted out and hooked up.

I then had to go for a CT scan. A doctor took me around with two nurses. We were near a door at the A&E department and as the door would open the rain would come in. I hadn't felt a cold breeze or rain on my face in over five weeks. I was happy to lay there and feel it and thank my lucky stars that I was still here. I went back to the ward to sleep for the rest of the day and through the night. I awoke to the newspapers in outrage at our fans and recognised some pals who would be looking at a little holiday after the 1.0 defeat.

I was caught between two outlooks daily. While feeling blessed and thankful to be alive, I would also slip into frustration about the prospect of being stuck in hospital for months rehabilitating.

I was missing Millwall and what a warm JD, dog burger from the van and a goalless draw would have done for my spirits, shouldn't be underestimated. One of my pals, Glassborow, wrote to the club telling them I had been through a shit few months and I think the players knew something was up because I hadn't been a string on the ponce for football memorabilia for a few months. The club wrote me a letter signed by all the players and at the bottom it had a message saying *'Get yourself fit as we want to give you a VIP day out at The Den soon'*. Every night I would look at that and see David Forde, Jimmy Abdou and Danny Shittu had signed it and like a kid I would smile. The next day, somehow, I would find the determination to push on a bit more.

I've always had to be determined and every day would require me to push on. So while I was confident of being able to get myself back to the levels I was pre trachi, I knew I had a difficult few weeks of rehabilitation at the Lane Fox Unit as I was told I may not eat, drink or talk at the same level as before. I needed to find out where I was as a person and I was desperate to know. I set myself a challenging regime of at first getting up, then every day staying up for an extra twenty minutes. Kellie would push me each day with a new task, maybe writing a letter or reading my book for a bit. I thrived on this and in fact this was the easy part, as I could see some kind of progress.

What I needed was a record of my progress as there were a couple of days when I didn't reach the targets I had set myself. The mist would come down, the mood would start and I was a total pain to be around. Once everyone went home, I knew it and I needed a tool to remind me of how well I was doing.

This may seem a bit silly but, by now, I'm now in this hospital for six weeks and I need a way of measuring my progress. Everyone was telling me I was doing superbly but I needed more. So I gave Kellie a list. Two simple online orders. A set of darts and a West Ham United calendar. The brief was clear, once the calendar arrived it would go on my wall near my hospital bed and at the end of each day Kellie would reward me with a dart for achieving my targets, two if I had overly achieved and three for some outstanding effort or breaking some personal bests.

It gets better, as by luck it was a Mark Noble calendar, come on, there can't be many people who wouldn't enjoy chucking a dart at his head!

This worked a treat and by writing on the calendar how many darts I had chucked the day before enabled me to track my progress and more importantly on the days I was disappointed with myself I could still put my progress into perspective and I got back up to speed a lot quicker than anyone would have believed, especially my doctors.

The calendar is still in our house somewhere. I think a few medical professionals were impressed but let's be honest, most thought I was a loon and I suppose I can't ever underestimate the small part Mark Noble played in my recovery.

By now I had started to notice so many improvements in my physical health since I had received the trachi. With so much down time all these improvements seemed magnified as I had so much time to reflect on them. I felt very positive about pushing myself on to overcome more challenges in the future. My breathing was so much stronger and I just felt so refreshed and energetic to the point my stamina went through the roof. I no longer felt tired around 3pm every day. My appetite returned and I had lost so much weight in the previous five years. Meal times when you are sick are a chore. They are not something you look forward to or enjoy, even if it is your favourite food. Now I was constantly hungry and also constantly snacking. But my greatest new trick wasn't a surprise. I was told by a couple of nurses that I would be able to kiss for longer now I had the trachi. One evening I was getting ready to change for bed. I was on my bed and Kellie was about to go. The curtains were around so we had some semi privacy. I pulled her towards me and kissed her. We kissed for what seemed like an age. I felt like Mouth from The Goonies or someone from American Pie, one of those cheeky characters from a distant film memory, the types who had been chasing that first kiss for a lifetime. This is the effect it had on me. It felt so, so real, even that dreaded "normal" word.

Let me out of here to put these skills to work. These attributes that I've rediscovered are like an old friend.

On Thursday 20.06.2013. I was finally discharged from hospital after being there for over thirteen weeks. I came home to a wife who had somehow got me through this, a large JD, chicken jalfrezi for dinner and two tickets that had arrived that day for the forthcoming Ashes Test Match at Lords. Life was fucking good again and once home it was time to concentrate on getting my mum home and healthy. By the time I was discharged she had managed to contract an infection and was back in Guy's Hospital. She was back in and I was getting out. I knew it would be hard to get her up straight, but I never knew at this point that our family's nightmare was far from over and that 2013 was certainly going to be my Annus Horribilis...

To Be

Continued...

Books by Lee Evans

I'm Still Standing

Staying Alive

Facebook: Lee Evans Author